THE NEW ASSISTIVE TECH

MAKE LEARNING AWESOME FOR ALL!

CHRISTOPHER R. BUGAJ

International Society for Technology in Education
PORTLAND, OREGON • ARLINGTON, VA

The New Assistive Tech
Make Learning Awesome for All!
Christopher R. Bugaj

© 2018 International Society for Technology in Education

Acquisitions and Developmental Editor: *Valerie Witte*
Copy Editor: *Jennifer Weaver-Neist*
Proofreader: *Steffi Drewes*
Indexer: *Wendy Allex*
Book Design and Production: *Kim McGovern*
Cover Design: *Eddie Ouellette*

Library of Congress Cataloging-in-Publication Data

Names: Bugaj, Christopher R. author. | International Society for Technology in Education.
Title: The new assistive technology : make learning awesome for all! / Christopher Bugaj.
Description: First Edition. | Portland, Oregon : International Society for Technology in Education, [2018] | Includes bibliographical references and index.
Identifiers: LCCN 2017057712 (print) | LCCN 2018019782 (ebook) | ISBN 9781564846846 | ISBN 9781564846839 | ISBN 9781564846853 | ISBN 9781564846884
Subjects: LCSH: Children with disabilities—Education—Computer-assisted instruction. | Self-help devices for people with disabilities. | Special education—Technological innovations. | Students with disabilities—Services for.
Classification: LCC LC4024 (ebook) | LCC LC4024 .B84 2018 (print) | DDC 371.33—dc23
LC record available at https://lccn.loc.gov/2017057712

First Edition
ISBN: 978-1-56484-688-4
Ebook version available

Printed in the United States of America

ISTE® is a registered trademark of the International Society for Technology in Education.

About ISTE

The International Society for Technology in Education (ISTE) is the premier nonprofit organization serving educators and education leaders committed to empowering connected learners in a connected world. ISTE serves more than 100,000 education stakeholders throughout the world.

ISTE's innovative offerings include the ISTE Conference & Expo, one of the biggest, most comprehensive edtech events in the world—as well as the widely adopted ISTE Standards for learning, teaching, and leading in the digital age and a robust suite of professional learning resources, including webinars, online courses, consulting services for schools and districts, books, and peer-reviewed journals and publications. Visit iste.org to learn more.

Join Our Community of Passionate Educators

ISTE members get free year-round professional development opportunities and discounts on ISTE resources and conference registration. Membership also connects you to a network of educators who can instantly help with advice and best practices.

Join or renew your ISTE membership today!

Visit iste.org/membership or call 1.800.336.5191.

Related ISTE Titles

The Practical (and Fun) Guide to Assistive Technology in Public Schools: Building or Improving Your District's AT Team, by Christopher R. Bugaj and Sally Norton-Darr

Dive into UDL: Immersive Practices to Develop Expert Learners, by Kendra Grant and Luis Perez

To see all books available from ISTE, please visit iste.org/resources.

About the Author

Christopher R. Bugaj, MA, CCC–SLP is a founding member of the assistive technology team for Loudoun County Public Schools. Chris hosts *The A.T.TIPSCAST* (attipscast.com), an award-winning podcast featuring strategies to design educational experiences. Chris is the coauthor of *The Practical (and Fun) Guide to Assistive Technology in Public Schools* published by the International Society for Technology in Education (ISTE) and has designed and instructed online courses for ISTE on the topics of assistive technology and Universal Design for Learning. He is also the author of ATEval2Go (bit.ly/ateval2go), an iPad app that helps professionals in education perform technology assessments for students. Chris coauthored two chapters for a book published by Brookes Publishing titled *Technology Tools for Students with Autism*. Chris coproduces and coauthors the popular *Night Light Stories* podcast (nightlightstories.net), which features original stories for children of all ages. Chris has presented over 250 live or digital sessions at local, regional, state, national, and international events, including TEDx, all of which are listed at bit.ly/bugajpresentations.

Acknowledgments

A book cannot be written unless the author has experiences about which to write. Throughout my career so far, I've been fortunate to work with passionate individuals who tirelessly dedicate their time, effort, and enthusiasm to improving the lives of others. These colleagues serve as teammates who cohesively bond together to make the world a better place by transforming educational practices day by day, student by student. On every team that I serve, I witness caring, compassion, innovation, and determination. To all of the educational experience designers of Loudoun County Public Schools, I thank you. Thank you for shaping my experiences and making them overwhelmingly positive! Without the moments we've shared together over the past 18 years, this book would not have been possible.

A book is not the work of the author alone. An entire publishing team of individuals at the International Society for Technology in Education took on the challenge of creating this book. Their expertise, input, and influence turned my rough words on a page into a work of art for the masses. Thank you for exceeding every expectation! Your skills and talents shine through!

A book sometimes has pictures, and this is one of those books! Thank you to the good people at toondoo.com and pixton.com for allowing me to use their tools to create comics included in this book.

A book takes gobs of time to write. The minutes spent writing a book is time the author isn't doing dishes, folding laundry, playing games, building forts, making dinners, going on hikes, or doing any of the other thousands of things that could be done with that time. If it weren't for the dedication, persistence, independence, and sacrifice of my family, this book wouldn't exist. Melissa, Tucker, and Margaret: thank you for your undying support!

Dedication

Time is limited by quantity—it is the one resource we can never replenish. You only get this one moment at this one time. If you have ever spent your valuable time listening to a single episode of the A.T.TIPSCAST, I thank you. If it weren't for your unending support, this podcast, which I've had the honor of hosting, would have probably ended back in 2009 or 2010. Listeners like you kept the fires burning long past what I thought possible. And if it weren't for you, I'm quite sure I would not have spent the time it took to author this book.

It was you who inspired me in ways unimaginable. Your impact on my life has been so immense that it cannot be quantified. Your influence, generosity, and spirit cannot be overstated. I appreciate all I've learned from you.

Thank you for listening, providing feedback, and sharing with others. This book is dedicated to you! And I look forward to spending more time together.

Contents

PART I
Education Re-Envisioned

CHAPTER 1
Shifting Attitudes to Improve Learning Experiences

CHAPTER 2
Personalized Learning Empowers *All* Students

CHAPTER 3
Considerations for Students with Disabilities

PART II
How to Consider Assistive Technology for Everybody

CHAPTER 4
Assistive Technology (Re)Defined

Foreword

Back in the day (really, did I say that?), when technology in education was more of a notion than a reality, I was lucky enough to be among a relatively small group of trailblazers who experienced first-hand the potential of technology to make a difference in the education and lives of people with disabilities. My personal experience was largely in the education sector, and I was thrilled by ways in which technology provided me with windows into what my students knew and were able to do. What I saw in my students raised my expectations for them and, through the use of technology, my students met and exceeded those expectations on a regular basis. It felt magical!

Back then, we were thrilled by the Individuals with Disabilities Education Act (IDEA) and other legislation that brought attention to the potential for technology to make a difference in the lives of students with disabilities by including language related to assistive technology (AT). There were definitions of AT devices and services (that "any item," "any service" thing) and a mandate requiring that students with disabilities be provided with AT devices and services needed to increase, improve, or maintain their capabilities (the purpose of those "any" items and services). For IDEA to require that AT devices and services be provided if needed as a part of a student's special education, related services, or supplementary aids and services was a BIG DEAL! It gave us the opportunity to have conversations that invited others less passionate or, perhaps, less experienced, into a world of fascinating possibilities! And then, IDEA upped the ante with the requirement that the AT needs of every student with disabilities be considered in the development of Individualized Education Programs (IEPs), which led to many more inviting conversations.

But that was then and this is now!

Although the same legal definitions and requirements are in place and must still be followed, the landscape of technology in education has changed radically. Technology is everywhere! Most students routinely use technology as a part of their lives, both educationally and personally. Many educational materials are digital, and the accessibility of those materials is improving through the inclusion of options that broaden their use by students across a wide range of abilities and needs. The idea that technology that works for some could work for all, with or without the use of assistive technology, is moving closer to reality every day.

And it is into the "now" that Christopher Bugaj take us in this book! If you have had the pleasure of learning from Chris in live or online presentations, you will find that his delightful and engaging style shines in the pages of this book as he weaves together assistive tech, accessibility, UDL, personalized learning, and so much more. As you read you will find yourself pondering assistive technology in a whole new way—a way that fits the "now" and moves well beyond compliance with statutory requirements. You will find yourself affirmed, challenged, and entertained! You will find yourself agreeing heartily in some parts and saying, "What????" in others, but, if you read with an open mind and inquiring stance, you will be changed. And because YOU have changed, you will be equipped to change the lives of students, families, and your fellow professionals.

Read, learn, question, and—above all—enjoy!

> — *Joy Smiley Zabala, Ed.D., developer of the SETT Framework*
> *and co-founder of QIAT (Quality Indicators for Assistive Technology)*

Introduction

Whenever you find yourself on the side of the majority,
it is time to pause and reflect.

—MARK TWAIN

Well, you're in it now—you've started to read this book. Before you go any further you should know that the ideas presented might challenge some of your conventional thoughts about education, learning, and people in general.

Here's *your* challenge: be open to it. Don't reject whatever concept is being introduced because it doesn't jive with your past experiences or current point of view. Instead, consider the point of the message and ask yourself why someone else might have this perspective. Ponder it. Flip it around like it's a Rubik's Cube. Contemplate the significance. Challenge yourself to question what you believe to be true. Most importantly, open yourself up to the possibility of change. Do not let cognitive dissonance control you. Without change, there is no growth. Be bold and embrace it, transforming your thoughts, opinions, and actions for the better. You'll be glad you did.

Remember: students out there need you to be open to new possibilities, especially if the old methods aren't working for them.

What's It All About?

Dear Reader,

Hi! My name is Chris, and I'm the author of this book. I wanted to give you a quick introduction so you know what you're getting yourself into.

Our journey starts, dear reader, with a question: what is the process for the selection and implementation of technology for students with disabilities in your neck of the woods?

This book primarily focuses on how to develop a consistent approach for choosing technology to design accessible, inclusive, and awesome educational experiences for the benefit of *all* students in public schools. Any educator interested in improving her or his practice will learn via these pages how planning for students with disabilities from the start can assist every other student.

The bulk of the content is aimed at support personnel whose primary responsibility is to help facilitate inclusive practices using technology. Traditionally, this has been someone working exclusively in special education who might have the term *assistive technology* (or *AT*) somewhere in their title.

Do you consider yourself an "AT Person?" If so, this book is for you!

Do you work to educate students with disabilities using technology? This book is for you too!

Do you want to coach other people to design accessible experiences which students and teachers alike think are great? OMG! You're holding the book you need right now!

The first part of *The New Assistive Tech* focuses on the adoption of contemporary educational practices and how they support students with disabilities. The book then shifts gears to discuss how support personnel can build capacity by assisting educators in making educational experiences accessible and inclusive through a process of technology consideration. The book goes on to explore a proactive approach to shifting the organization rigidity of the educational institution to one of agility and flexibility by increasing professional development and by developing a plan of action for systemic change. If you work—in any capacity—to support students with disabilities, this book is for you!

By the end of this book, you'll have learned the following:

- How embracing student-centered, contemporary education philosophies such as Project-Based Learning and Growth Mindset works to support students with disabilities.

- How to plan and execute educational experiences using technology centered around the needs of students with disabilities.

- How to effectively and consistently consider and select technological supports based on the specific needs of an individual student with a disability.

- How to assist an Individualized Education Program team when they need help determining which supports to put in place for a student with a disability.

- How to approach providing professional development and training on accessible and inclusive practices to other educators in your educational institution (and beyond).

- How to develop a customized plan of action for developing a culture of inclusivity and accessibility specific to the needs of your educational institution.

Thank you for your willingness to dive deeper as we explore methodologies that can bring about the systemic changes necessary to transform education into something awesome for everybody, including students with disabilities.

Your buddy,

Chris

Connecting to the ISTE Educator Standards

This book is published by the International Society for Technology in Education, which has these amazing sets of standards for students, educators, coaches, and administrators. These standards provide an outline of the skills and traits students will need in the future. They apply to everyone working in education, including students with disabilities and those educators working to support them. Each chapter references how its content aligns with one or more of the ISTE Standards for Educators, although connections overlap with the student, coach, and administrator standards as well. The ISTE Standards for Educators encourage educators to model learning for students, to seek out leadership opportunities, to contribute productively as global citizens, to collaborate to solve authentic problems, to design powerful educational experiences for everyone, and to facilitate the integration of technology to support student-centered achievements. The standards apply to this book's central idea, which is to select and utilize technology to actualize the potential of every student.

Things to Know Before You Begin

This book is meant to be enjoyable to read—as opposed to a slog that you force yourself to get through. To help you along the way, I've included true-to-life stories based on my experiences in education, fictional parables meant to provide meaningful analogies, and other fun bits like songs and rhymes to reinforce what you learn. Engagement is a necessary consideration in any educational experience, and these stylistic elements are intended to provide an engaging educational experience for you. More importantly, though, the book is meant to empower you to act.

As the reader, you might find yourself skipping around from chapter to chapter or part to part as you find what resonates with you. The hope is that you will flag intriguing portions of the book for your own reference and then use the portions you flagged to change minds and influence others toward positive change. I hope you find yourself saying something like, "See? It's right here in this book. Let's do this!"

Tips from the Author

Throughout the book, you'll find handy messages called Awesome Insights with bite-sized chunks of information that give quick pointers or suggestions to contemplate. Look for them throughout the book for useful hints, tips, and other ideas to ponder.

Join the Community and Stay Connected

Reading this book makes you part of a larger community. Join the conversation by using the hashtag #AwesomeAT4All on all social media outlets, liking the Facebook page at facebook.com/awesomeatforall, and checking out the online compendium at bit.ly/newatbooksite. As part of your experience, the book is interspersed with hyperlinks to more content, and each one (along with a few fun extras) is included in the compendium. In addition to the link above, you can access the site by using this QR code.

Key Terms

Here are a few important terms to know as you read through the book:

Accessible. Accessibility is a characteristic or quality of a product, service, or location that allows this product, service, or location to be used. Anything created is accessible to some people. "Accessible" is a synonym for the word "usable," but usability is relative, as physical, verbal, visual, auditory, and cognitive abilities vary from person to person. If the creator wants the creation to be used by the largest number of people, then the creation needs to be created with variability in mind. The more usable a creation is, the more accessible it becomes. In this book (and beyond), when discussing making, providing, or choosing materials for people of varying abilities, the term "accessible" really means "accessible to the widest range of abilities" or "accessible to the largest number of people."

Disability. For the purposes of this book, the term "disability" is defined using the definition outlined in the Individuals with Disabilities Education Improvement Act (Public Law 108-446), which states that a child with a disability is one "with mental retardation, hearing impairments (including deafness), speech or language impairments, visual impairments (including blindness), serious emotional disturbance (referred to in this title as 'emotional disturbance'), orthopedic impairments, autism, traumatic brain injury, other health impairments, or specific learning disabilities; and (ii) who, by reason thereof, needs special education and related services."

Educational agency. Educational agency? School district? Academic institution? School system? What do you call the organization where educators work? These terms are used interchangeably for the purposes of this book, referring to a place— no matter how big or how small—where learning is supposed to happen.

Individualized Education Program (IEP). In the United States, an Individualized Education Program is a federally mandated document drafted by stakeholders invested in a student with a disability. At a minimum, it is reviewed annually.

Professional development (PD). Think of educators learning new technologies, strategies, interventions, philosophies, and any other techniques to further their own knowledge and skills.

Technology. This is a synonym for "tools." Although it might conjure pictures of something electronic, it doesn't necessarily need to be an item that runs on electricity. A wheel, for instance, is technology that makes things move but doesn't necessarily need to be attached to a motor for it to work. The term "technology," when applied in an educational context, is any tool that helps a student learn.

PART 1

EDUCATION RE-ENVISIONED

CHAPTER 1

Shifting Attitudes to Improve Learning Experiences

In any good book, there is conflict. The protagonist faces some sort of challenge to overcome. This book is no different, except here, *you* are the protagonist; *you* are the hero of the story. The challenge is to imagine the experience of school in new way: imagine every student, with or without disabilities, choosing to be at school over any other activity. This chapter explores steps that can be taken toward that end.

Advances in technology provide educators with the opportunity to design every learning experience with individual needs in mind. These changes have led to revolutionary ideas that have made educators reconsider common practices and rethink what education really means.

Let's begin by diving headlong into how contemporary philosophies, initiatives, and practices positively impact and influence the instruction of students with disabilities. In this chapter, you'll:

1. Learn how to shift student and educator perspectives on school from a place where one *needs* to be to a place one *wants* to be.

2. Examine how traditional practices in school impact the attitudes of students toward learning—especially those students with disabilities.

3. Explore how to reshape and rethink what it means to be a teacher by rebranding the profession.

4. Learn a short process for designing inclusive, accessible, student-centered learning experiences.

ISTE STANDARDS ADDRESSED

ISTE Standards for Educators 2b. Advocate for equitable access to educational technology, digital content, and learning opportunities to meet the diverse needs of all students.

ISTE Standards for Educators 3a. Create experiences for learners to make positive, socially responsible contributions and exhibit empathetic behaviors online that build relationships and community.

ISTE Standards for Educators 5a. Use technology to create, adapt, and personalize learning experiences that foster independent learning and accommodate learner differences and needs.

ISTE Standards for Educators 5b. Design authentic learning activities that align with content-area standards, and use digital tools and resources to maximize active, deep learning.

ISTE Standards for Educators 5c. Explore and apply instructional design principles to create innovative digital learning environments that engage and support learning.

ISTE Standards for Educators 6a. Foster a culture where students take ownership of their learning goals and outcomes in both independent and group settings.

ISTE Standards for Educators 6d. Model and nurture creativity and creative expression to communicate ideas, knowledge, and/or connections.

The Like–Dislike Continuum Activity

Let's do an activity. In the space below, list five things in the world that are generally liked—or even loved—by most people. Now, these things can't be stuff we need in order to survive as humans, like water or food, but they can be types of drinks or food (like chocolate). Again, these are things that most people really, really, *really* like. (And it's totally okay to write in this book [or to annotate it if you're reading an ebook version] because it is your copy!)

Got your five things that people, universally, seem to like? Great! Now, let's do another five. This time, however, let's do five things that humans, in general, don't like. Document those five items in the space below using any method that works for you.

Likes	Dislikes
1.	1.
2.	2.
3.	3.
4.	4.
5.	5.

Now, let's combine the lists and then sort the items, ranking the items that people, according to you, like the most (number 1) to what they like the least (number 10). Take your time and think about it. Feel free to go back and adjust your answers above if need be. We want to make sure this list feels accurate to you, as we're going to use it later as a basis for measuring other items.

1. *(Most liked)*

2.

3.

4.

5. *(Generally liked)*

6. *(Generally disliked)*

7.

8.

9.

10.   *(Most disliked)*

What you've just built is a scale by which you can measure any concept to see how much you think the general population enjoys it. For example, imagine most students attending school. Ask yourself, "Where do students rank school on my 10-item scale of likes and dislikes?"

Now, take away the social component of school and only consider the academic aspects of it. Does that change the ranking at all?

This activity has been done with educators many times in live and virtual events. The ranking of "school" is almost always the same, with people placing it somewhere between root canals and mosquito bites, or between sunburns and traffic jams. Some educators are adamant that most students would rank school near 9 or 10 in the realm of disease, natural disasters, and death. Although there are students who are exceptions, a general agreed-upon principle is that school, to put it simply, sucks.

Students tend to equate school with something one just needs to get through: a drudgery, a slog, a grind. Graduation parties tend to celebrate an escape to freedom, like getting out of prison, rather than a celebration of the academic experiences had. This negative connotation for school is held by most students, regardless of ability.

Most students do not have a disability. In fact, according to the National Center for Education Statistics, approximately 13 percent of the student population has a disability (bit.ly/ncesdisabilitystatistics). Imagine how much less enjoyable school might be if you had a physical, sensory, cognitive, or language-based disability in an educational environment where the experience is not necessarily designed with you in mind.

Now, let's consider most educators. Where do they put school on your scale? Take away the fact that an educator is being paid to be there. Take away summer breaks too. Consider just the day-to-day actions of an educator. Where does school fall?

Ask the next 10 educators you meet how they are doing, and you'll probably hear phrases like, "I'm hanging in there," "It's almost Friday," "Is it break yet?", "I'm getting by," and a slew of other phrases that express frustration, aggravation, and annoyance. It's rare that you hear how great everything is, how much they love their jobs, and how they can't wait to be back the next day.

Now, imagine you're an educator who works primarily in special education. The turnover rates for a special-education teacher are very high, with an attrition rate averaging approximately 13 percent per year (McLeskey, Tyler, & Flippin, 2004). The attrition rate of special educators moving to general education positions is more than 10 times larger than general educators transferring into special-education positions (McLeskey et al., 2004). Using this turnover rate as one metric, the number of people who last in special education is lower than that of teachers working primarily in general education.

The cultural perspectives on school in the United States, whether from educators or students, regardless of ability, are almost universally bleak. It is time to change school into something everyone deems as a positive experience.

Snow Day!

In certain parts of the United States the months between November and March are filled with a magical sense of hope and wonder. Students and educators alike become sorcerers, wizards, and witches casting spells and concocting potions to influence the weather. Some flush ice cubes (only three!) down the toilet. Others dance around in their kitchens wearing blue-and-white pajamas inside out. Still others freeze a spoon (or a white crayon) and place it under their pillows. These rituals are performed with great care and precision in the hopes of summoning Jack Frost into action. If successful, he will answer desperate prayers by creating a storm so treacherous that officials will cancel school. When that call comes, the radiating elation is so immense, it can melt an iceberg!

Why is it that those who attend and work in a school are so overjoyed to have a temporary reprieve from the environment in which they spend seven hours a day?

No matter how much they love what they are doing, everyone enjoys a day off—a day free of obligations and responsibilities. Right?

Maybe not.

What if the experience of school was so amazing that students and teachers felt sadness rather than happiness when notified of a snow day? What if students and teachers everywhere loved the experience of school so much that they practiced rituals to keep inclement weather at bay rather than embracing their inner Elsa? What if, as a culture, closing school for a day brought about feelings of disappointment at what wouldn't be accomplished that day rather than pure bliss at what would be avoided? What if students craved school because they knew that attendance on that day meant they'd be working toward making a meaningful contribution to society by attempting to solve some problem plaguing the lives of others?

Wouldn't everyone be happier if students and teachers enjoyed the school experience so much that they desperately wanted to be there? This shift in thinking can be achieved—but it won't be fairy or elven magic that changes this perspective. Like the accumulation of billions of snowflakes, this change can only happen over time through people, just like you, designing awesome experiences. Technology can help too! Thanks to your efforts, when a storm is brewing but a school remains open, people will consider it the most wonderful time of the year.

Name This Disability

Figure 1.1 is a worksheet that contains printed questions about content related to science, such as the properties of matter. Below each question is a space for a student to handwrite a response. The student has attempted to answer each question, but the legibility is questionable. Erratic letter formation, size, spacing, and alignment make the words and sentences difficult to decode.

Using the description and any other powers of observation and resources at your disposal, answer this question: What disability does this student have? (Dyslexia? Dysgraphia? A visual impairment? A physical impairment that impacts motor function of the upper extremities? Multiple disabilities? What do you think?)

The answer is that this work was produced by a typically developing student in sixth grade with no known disability.

Concerns abound with this example but not regarding the student's abilities or learning. Instead, the concerns center around the design of the lesson, the teacher's expectation, and the materials presented. Did the experience of completing this activity help the student fall in love with the content or has repeated participation in activities like this pushed the enjoyment of science further away? After completing the assignment, does the student feel a sense of pride in the work done and the learning that has taken place? Does this activity consider the needs of each individual student or was every student in the class given the same sheet with the same expectation to complete it in the same way?

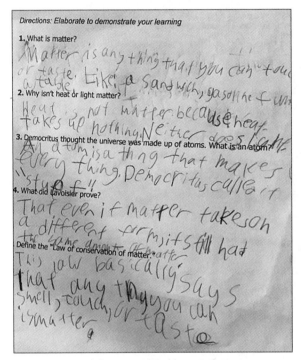

Figure 1.1 A worksheet completed by a student.

Do discouraging experiences like the one above make up the majority or minority of this student's time spent in school? Does this student's experience vary greatly from the experience of other students around the United States (or the world)? Does this experience foster creativity, collaboration, critical thinking, or any of the other skills necessary to prepare students for the future (such as those outlined in the ISTE Standards at the beginning of this chapter)?

You be the judge. (See Figures 1.2 and 1.3.)

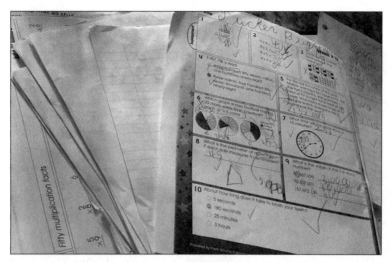

Figure 1.2 Articles taken from a student's backpack at the end of any given week.

Figure 1.3 To the recycling bin on the last day of school!

A EULOGY FOR WORKSHEETS

Today, we gather to pay our respects to a staple of the school-based environment for decades: worksheets. Everyone knows worksheets—they've shaped hearts and minds for generations. Assigning a worksheet as a way for students to demonstrate what they've learned has ensured hours of peaceful activity, keeping most students quiet and still. Completion of a worksheet has helped students feel that sense of accomplishment in starting something, answering questions, and then finishing it. Countless students have experienced the joy of expanding their working memory through the task of temporarily memorizing facts to complete blank spaces and then abandoning those facts before they could take root to corrupt their long-term memories.

Worksheets were everyone's friend. Students would wake in the morning eager and enthusiastic to spend the precious hours of their youth in school, completing worksheets. Because of worksheets, many students experienced the endorphin-fueled rush that came from seeing a high percentage scribbled at the top of a page, grading their efforts. How many times has elation washed over a student as he or she found the crumpled remains of an overdue worksheet at the bottom of a school bag, thought to be lost forever?

Worksheets endured the pain of erratic penmanship to convey streams of consciousness for educators to sometimes read, return to weeks later, and then ultimately file in the circular cabinet. In the days since worksheets have passed, the world has seen an increase in student confusion. If not ordered to complete worksheets, how are they to spend their time?

The monumental impact of worksheets on shaping the mindset of the future cannot be overstated. Student after student learned repeatedly, through the completion of worksheets, that life's decisions are either correct or incorrect— literally black or white. They developed a passion for science, mathematics, art, and all the other areas of study, not through real-world application with real-world consequences but through banal yet measured perseverance. Without work-sheets, students will now need different opportunities to learn grit and dogged determination.

With worksheets gone, educators are concerned that they won't have an opportu-nity to practice their technological repair skills. Wrestling with paper jams in copy machines was a mainstay for how educators learned critical troubleshooting skills. Moreover, gone are the days of waiting for the copy machine to be free, resulting in a decreased likelihood of chance encounters with colleagues. With worksheets gone, educators must be diligent in using the lost time at copy machines on other collaborative endeavors or suffer the fate of attrition.

The lack of printer use and the cessation of the continuous supply of ink to fuel them will cause a decrease in expenditures. With those line items in a school's operating budget gone, administrators will reel as they attempt to discover what to do with those extra funds. Don't administrators have enough to do without shouldering this extra burden?

With worksheets having moved on to the great paper pile in the sky, we will all need to chart a new course through these open waters. With the absence of worksheets, educators are struggling to answer pressing questions: In a world devoid of simulated problems whose answers are handwritten on worksheets, how will students practice problem-solving skills? How will students know the one right answer? How will educators check for student understanding of content? What types of other formative assessments can be used to assess students as easily, efficiently, and accurately as a worksheet? How will students be graded on their performance and understand their worth? How will students with reading and writing difficulties even know they have these difficulties without being presented with a worksheet? How will students who really enjoyed filling out worksheets (which are most) have an opportunity to shine above the few who struggled?

With worksheets gone, the world of education will change forever.

Goodbye, dear friend. Your impacts were felt far and wide. Rest in peace.

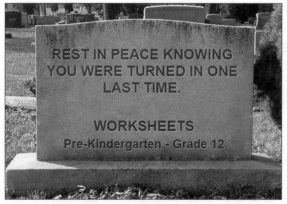

Figure 1.4 Thanks for the memories…
(Made using tombgen.appspot.com)

What's in a Name?

Have you ever wondered how different your life might be if your parents had simply chosen a different name for you? Might you be in an entirely different place, doing different things, engaging with different people if your name were Owen rather than Tucker, or Loretta rather than Margaret?

The words we choose matter. The very words you are reading right now have been carefully chosen to make a point. If the wrong words are selected, intention and meaning could be misconstrued. The words we use help define who we are and what we stand for.

We use words to instruct students. A large part of any subject is simply learning the vocabulary used. What do you do when you don't know what a word means? A contemporary answer would be to search for the term on the internet.

For instance, do you know what a quokka is? An online image search immediately generates an array of pictures providing a quick visual definition. The collage from different sources helps one understand how a culture defines the word.

Figure 1.5 A quokka is a small mammal located exclusively on Rottnest Island, off the coast of Perth in Australia.

Definitions take root in our brain and shape our reality. What type of image is conjured in the heads of those who hear or read a particular word?

Let's try an exercise. I'm going to give you a word and ask you to conjure an image of what it means in your mind. Once you read the word, take a moment to put down the book, close your eyes, and visualize how you might represent the word as an image. Resist the temptation to keep reading past the word. Instead, stop, take a moment, and let the image take shape. Consider the characteristics of what you see in your mind's eye.

Ready? Here's the word…

teacher

What did you see? What does a contemporary teacher look like to you?

With that in mind, let's do another exercise. Do an online image search for the word *teacher*. You will likely find images of people—predominantly women—standing in front of a chalkboard, perhaps pointing at something on the board. Many will be smiling, joyously going about their business of pouring knowledge into the open minds of adoring students. Most images involve the teacher being in front of students who are seated in rows of desks. Many of the images will show the teacher standing over the students, physically above them in space.

Now, compare the results of what you found when you did the image search to the one you conjured of a contemporary teacher in your own mind. Is it the same? If an image search is reflective of society's view of a concept, then what does that say for the meaning of *teacher*? Does contemporary pedagogical practice reflect the collage of images? Do contemporary teachers stand in front of chalkboards? Are teachers, the holders of the Cup of Knowledge, graciously bestowing it upon their willing, thirsty pupils? Even if the image search does reflect your current vision of teaching, the next logical question might be whether this is what you want it to represent.

Words come and go with time. For example, words like *groovy* are replaced with others like *rad*, which are, in turn, replaced with new words, like *awesome*. Perhaps it's time the word *teacher* takes its turn on the backburner of English parlance due to its entrenched legacy in society.

What shifts would take place in the practice of education and in the very culture it works to construct if we simply changed the name of the occupation? If not *teacher*, then what should we call those in the noble profession of educating others? What term would evoke imagery of contemporary practices in which educators guide students to take responsibility for their own learning?

The term should immediately invite those entering the profession to place the diversity of their students at the forefront of their minds. It should place the student, rather than the curriculum, at the center of the model of education. It should reflect the idea that the instructor's role is to create an environment rather than deliver content. The term should propagate the idea that curiosity, discovery, and a passion for knowing the truth brings about deep fulfillment in life. It should be strong and commanding, and imbue a sense of responsibility in constructing an atmosphere where students can collaborate, communicate, and create solutions by critically thinking about authentic problems. The term should reflect guidance over dictation and cooperation over compliance. The term should embody the notion that students learn best when they are trusted, empowered, invested, and having fun.

Instead of the word *teacher*, educators will hereby be known as:

educational experience designers

Qualities of an Educational Experience Designer

An educational experience designer is one who embraces these principles:

- Guides (doesn't dictate)
- Expects, welcomes, and plans for the diverse needs of learners
- Models flexibility
- Encourages movement
- Takes chances
- Understands that trying but failing means growth
- Uses technology to provide options

Designing Better Educational Experiences for Everyone

As discussed at the beginning of this chapter, students often perceive the act of going to school in negative terms; and for a student with a disability, this perception might be even worse. One way to make learning more enjoyable is to fundamentally alter the experience by designing it differently. One giant step in that direction would be for those who teach to start considering themselves educational experience designers. As a designer of educational experiences that students will enjoy, the starting point is the consideration of how those with differing abilities will interact in that experience. And technology should be considered in this design process to help provide a varied educational experience for all the different individuals participating.

Three Phases of Educational Experience Design

Traditionally, when a teacher plans a lesson, he or she starts by examining a standard and asking, "How am I going to teach this standard to the class?" An educational experience designer starts by asking, "How am I going to design experiences where each student discovers the purpose of the standard?" For example, instead of the thinking, "How am I going to present information about the solar system to the class?" the educational experience designer asks, "What are the different questions, problems, stories, events, and other techniques that will intrigue each student into wanting to own learning about the solar system?"

Designing an educational experience can be broken down into three phases (see Figure 1.6). During each phase, the educational experience designer begins the process by anticipating how each individual student will be invested in the examination of the content.

Planning

The educational experience designer works alone or with a team to plan the experience for students with specific attention paid to the learning needs of students with disabilities. Pedagogical evidence mixed with practical application and imagination are used to develop the methods used in the experience. Materials (including technology) are acquired during this phase that might be used during the experience to ensure that every student can access the content. Educational experience designers plan with flexibility in mind, leading with the idea that their educational experiences are so inclusive and accessible, they will rarely—if ever—need to be modified.

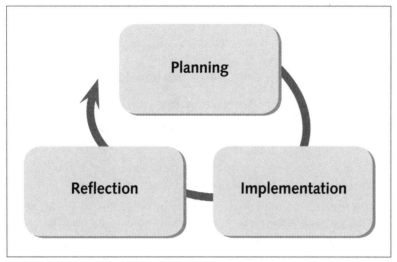

Figure 1.6 Three phases of educational experience design: (1) planning,
(2) implementation, and (3) reflection.

When planning, the educational experience designer considers:

- Which questions will engage, inspire, and empower each student to take action to learn the content?

- Which technology can be made available to remove any potential barriers to accessing the content with specific regard to the varied abilities of each student?

- What are acceptable ways for each student to demonstrate that learning has occurred?

Implementation

The planned experience occurs, but an educational experience designer rarely leads the experience by directing learners through an explicit set of directives with which everyone must comply. Instead, educational experience designers offer guidance to students as they work through the process of exploring the content. The educational experience designer helps students make connections in understanding, asking probing questions, suggesting tools and resources, and answering questions as students go through their own process of learning. As the experience progresses, adjustments are made wherever necessary. The educational experience designer and, when possible, the student gather data and evidence on outcomes. During the implementation phase, the educational experience designer considers:

- How can I best initiate the experience with each learner?

- How can I make adjustments when the experience is not going as planned?

- How can I guide each student to make connections with the content being learned?

Reflection

Each student analyzes the data and outcomes that were collected during the implementation phase of the experience and reflects on her or his own learning. The data and evidence for each student is also reviewed by the educational experience designer (or a team of educational experience designers) to ensure that each student has made progress toward learning the content. If a student has a disability, this information is used to monitor progress toward the goals outlined on the Individualized Education Program (IEP). Each student also gives feedback to the educational experience designer about what worked and what could be improved. Reflection on the experience guides the practice for the next experience.

When reflecting, the educational experience designer considers:

- How can I help students determine the extent to which learning, progress, and growth has taken place?

- How can I help students examine which tools and resources ensured individual progress?

- How can I collect feedback from the student about how the experience impacted perceptions on the specific topic and facilitated a love of learning?

Student Choice

When a person seeks employment, they have a choice in what they'd like to do. On any given day, an educator can choose to pursue a different career path—educators have that choice. Students do not.

Educational experience designers recognize this reality for every student and use this awareness to consciously and intentionally make the whole experience of learning better. Rather than assigning tasks, educational experience designers offer invitations so empowering that students become invested in participation *by choice*. Educational experience designers present problems that entice students to use their abilities, whatever they may be, to make meaningful contributions to the world. During the time spent in school (and beyond), each student learns the content specified in the standards while enjoying the entire process.

Education is a never-ending journey driven largely by one's innate sense of discovery. School is a place. Education transcends school. Respecting, honoring, and fostering a student's innate drive to learn through encouragement and support is a necessary acknowledgment of an educational experience designer. The educational experience designer understands that the heart of learning is student choice. Therefore, when designing the experience, the educational experience designer provides students with authentic choices regarding the technology they'd like to use to engage in the act of learning. This is what student choice is all about. Students get to choose what they want to work on and how they want to work on it during their time spent in school.

AWESOME INSIGHT

Educational experience designers ask three fundamental questions when planning:

1. Is this an experience I would want to have myself?

2. Is this experience meaningful and purposeful to every participant?

And, most importantly...

3. Is it awesome?

The CURRE

How do you design inspiring educational experiences? Use this simple acronym—CURRE (aptly pronounced "cure")—as the magical elixir that prevents lesson plans from becoming "sick" in the first place.

C—Curiosity

Every human, despite ability or disability, attempts to figure out his or her environment. It doesn't matter if you have autism, multiple sensory impairments, physical disabilities, a disability that impacts cognition, or any combination of those (or if you don't have a disability at all). Everyone explores the world around them to the greatest extent possible. Educational experience designers tap into a student's innate sense of wonder to invite the student to explore his or her world further. Curiosity starts with mystery. Give students a mystery to solve and a question to answer.

U—Uniqueness

Build opportunities for individuals to shine. As an educational experience designer, plan for different ways for students to choose to show off individual talents. For example, some might choose to be the heavy lifters while others are the note takers, researchers, leaders, timekeepers and so on. If you expect every student to do the same thing the same way, you're forcing compliance rather than encouraging independence. That is the opposite of awesome. Provide options and structure flexibility into how students can experience the content by using the different technologies available. Highlight moments and choices made by students to show off their uniqueness in their use of whatever tools they choose.

R—Risk

Invite students to take chances. Trying out a potential solution that turns out to be a failure is part of learning. Analyzing what didn't work and why helps students learn how to approach the next problem they will face without (or with much less) trepidation. Invite students to try a technology that piques their interest and allows them to experience or create something without fear that the monsters of time, grades, and compliance will get in their way. Reward choices that require students to go out on a limb and push their boundaries. Provide guidance to help students examine why their choices did or did not work.

R—Real World

We all live in this world together; let's work together make it a better place. Students only get to be a certain age once, so make each year's experiences meaningful. Invite students to be the difference that changes the world. Look for opportunities to help others by working to solve social, economic, political, humanitarian, environmental, and cultural issues locally, regionally, nationally, or internationally. When students see they are making a difference, they will want to continue doing so, and learning will become habitual in the process.

E—Enjoyment

Make learning fun. Obviously, students don't have to be rolling on the floor laughing every minute of every class, but humor increases the enjoyment of the overall activity. Enhance the aspects of games and gamification whenever possible by injecting a spirit of joy and fun. If the designed experience is fun, students will stand a better chance of remembering and applying what they've learned.

With each exceptional experience that gets designed, the perception around school will change. How we think about school in our culture will start to shift—not just for students but for educators as well. Dread or malaise will be replaced by excitement and enthusiasm. When school is designed to be energizing, students will want to be there. And they'll want to be involved in designing their own experiences too.

Impact On Students with Disabilities

In any profession where a service or product is being created for a consumer, there is an element of design. To make that service or product appealing to the largest number of people, the designers must consider the needs of multiple individuals. Failure to consider how people with known disabilities will interact with your service or product would mean cutting out a potential user base right from inception. Those who design inclusively maximize the quantity of potential users.

Design innovation that benefits every user typically stems from attempts to remove a barrier for a person with disability. Later, this technology that was designed to help those with a disability often becomes a mainstream feature for the masses. Likewise, an educational experience designer knows and understands that constructing curriculum for students with disabilities—right from the onset—ultimately meets the needs of every other learner as well. (Examples and a process—with formulas and everything!—for applying technologies specifically designed to assist people with disabilities to the benefit of everyone else are outlined in chapter 10.)

Successful design is not predicated on adaptation. One does not start the design process by asking, "How can people with disabilities be included in this experience I already designed?" Instead, at inception, an educational experience designer asks the question, "How can I design this experience for every person, including those with disabilities?"

Consistently using this mode of thinking transforms one's perspective. When one attempts to put disability at the forefront of the design process, it becomes apparent that not all people have the same disability. For instance, if a person has a visual impairment, what this person needs to access his or her education might vary greatly from that of someone who has a hearing impairment. Therefore, successful educational design requires flexibility and variability. Providing options for how a student chooses to engage in the experience is a key element in successful educational design.

Plan with the End In Mind

It is easy to mistake progress for success. Unless a long-term vision and goal is set, it is entirely possible for a student to demonstrate steady progress on established yearly goals all year long but still not obtain an overarching goal in the end. For example, there are students who might have communication goals in which they are taught how to point to a picture to request an object with the idea that, someday, this will lead them to a more robust language system. All year long, given no other means or instruction, the student makes progress on more accurately pointing to pictures, but when graduation rolls around, that student might still be pointing to single pictures rather than having a developed, robust language system combining words for different purposes.

When Individualized Education Programs are reviewed annually (at a minimum) and the makeup of the team changes regularly, it can be difficult to keep the endgame in mind. Educational experience designers recognize this trap and work to avoid it by planning with the end in mind. They ask themselves, "What do I want this student to be capable of doing on his or her last day, when he or she leaves the local education agency? What skills will this student need to be successful in life?"

These are heavy, deep questions that cannot be shied away from. And you should answer these questions as early as possible, with unlimited expectations. Draft a plan including the choice of tools necessary to assist the student in achieving this result.

To further the example of a student working on communication goals, the team might decide that on the last day, they'd like for the student to have the skill of communicating for a variety of purposes by combining words using appropriate grammar and syntax. Knowing that this is the long-term desired result, the team selects a communication device with a robust language system, sets forth learning how to implement that system, and then integrates it into almost every action of every day.

Minute by minute, hour by hour, day by day, week by week, year by year, the student is exposed to and practices using the language system. Though success is not ensured for anyone and the student may still leave without having mastered this communication system, because the team had an exit strategy in mind from the onset, with a longer-term goal established early on, the chance for success is optimized.

Measuring Joy with Emotional Index Quotients

Contemporary society has means for rating experiences. When you truly have a wonderful time at a restaurant, show, or event, you have the opportunity to share your opinion with the wider world by writing a review, ranking it with a number of stars, or (at least) giving it a thumbs-up or -down. When considering the purchase of a product from any online retailer, for instance, one tool you have is to read the reviews for that product. The review helps protect the consumer while simultaneously providing feedback to the seller, creator, or designer on how the product or experience could be improved.

A similar system can be applied with students after an educational experience. They can be invited to rank the experience and provide feedback to the educational experience designer. A simple five-star or smiley-face ranking system could be employed, but other, possibly more relevant and fun options also exist. Symbols can associate with the school mascot, the content, or any other item of interest. Consider the open-source symbol sets from useiconic.com/open as options (Figure 1.7).

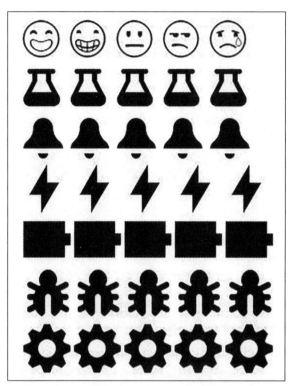

Figure 1.7 Consider using emojis, beakers, bells, flashes, batteries, insects, gears, or any other icons to help students provide feedback on their learning experiences.

Providing an opportunity to rate and comment on an experience has multiple benefits. Educational experience designers can use the score to create a quantitative measure that literally shows how much students are enjoying their learning experience. These cumulative and summative quantities can be presented alongside any other assessment measures used to evaluate educator, school, and/or district performance. Presenting the information alongside test-score data emphasizes the point that enjoying the experience is an equally valuable learning outcome. Most important, implementing a ranking system encourages students to reflect upon the learning experience, promoting the idea that the student is the one in charge of the learning.

May the Odds Be Ever In Your Favor

The act of learning is not a trial of endurance by which one proves moxie, grit, or stamina. Public education is not supposed to be a competition where only the strongest survive. School is not a contrived arena sport pitting youth against youth for the purposes of entertainment or control. Students are not tributes forced to do the commands of adults. The activity of learning does not equate to the Hunger Games.

In the United States, everyone has a right to a free appropriate public education (or FAPE, as outlined in section 504 of the Individuals with Disabilities Education Act), with equal access to materials. People from every district have a right to learn more to improve their own knowledge and skills in whatever subject area they choose. School, therefore, should be designed in such a way that the odds are ever in students' and teachers' favor. Anything less shifts the focus from the very people school is supposed to benefit: the students and, ultimately, society at large.

AWESOME INSIGHT

For a deeper overview of educational experience design, check out this video:

bit.ly/experiencedesigners

CHAPTER 2

Personalized Learning Empowers *All* Students

Some major educational philosophies and movements support the notion of designing educational experiences in schools that bring about a joy, respect, and love of learning for all, including those with disabilities. These movements are steeped in research and supported by governmental law. The convergence in everyday practice of these various philosophies can bring about sustainable change to education for everyone, including those with disabilities. The philosophies predominantly include Universal Design for Learning (UDL), Project-Based Learning (PBL), and Growth Mindset.

Personalized learning is a term that ties these individual philosophies together under one umbrella. The core ideal of personalized learning is that education should be student centered and driven rather than standardized for all. Using these principles to design instructional experiences for students with disabilities isn't exclusionary; all means *all*. These same principles can be used to design experiences for students whose disabilities might be considered more severe. Every student, no matter their abilities, deserves an education that is designed to meet their needs.

In this chapter, you'll:

1. Examine how the principles of Universal Design for Learning work in conjunction with other contemporary educational philosophies.

2. Discuss how the adoption of a Bring Your Own Device (BYOD) perspective positively promotes student choice by reinforcing the idea that the tools used in learning are personal.

3. Explore how Project-Based Learning improves educational experiences for students with and without disabilities.

4. Learn how the language and attitudes related to facilitating a Growth Mindset positively impacts students with and without disabilities.

ISTE STANDARDS ADDRESSED

ISTE Standards for Educators 2b. Advocate for equitable access to educational technology, digital content, and learning opportunities to meet the diverse needs of all students.

ISTE Standards for Educators 5a. Use technology to create, adapt, and personalize learning experiences that foster independent learning and accommodate learner differences and needs.

ISTE Standards for Educators 5b. Design authentic learning activities that align with content-area standards, and use digital tools and resources to maximize active, deep learning.

ISTE Standards for Educators 5c. Explore and apply instructional design principles to create innovative digital learning environments that engage and support learning.

ISTE Standards for Educators 6b. Manage the use of technology and student learning strategies in digital platforms, virtual environments, hands-on makerspaces, and/or in the field.

ISTE Standards for Educators 6d. Model and nurture creativity and creative expression to communicate ideas, knowledge, and/or connections.

ISTE Standards for Educators 7a. Provide alternative ways for students to demonstrate competency and reflect on their learning using technology.

Universal Design for Learning

The premise of this principle has its roots in architectural design. When constructing anything, you must design the structure in such a way that anyone can access it. Educators who embrace this philosophy do the same when building learning environments and when constructing the experiences happening in those learning environments. Those who subscribe to the principles of Universal Design for Learning (UDL) understand that everyone is different. UDL invites educators to provide options for how they represent content, multiple means for how students can express what they know, and the ability to create varied and engaging experiences.

Purveyors of Universal Design for Learning advocate for three pillars by which to construct learning experiences. One of these three pillars is Multiple Means of Representation, which indicates that educators should provide a variety of ways for students to experience content. Multiple Means of Action and Expression, another pillar, invites educators to create experiences where students express what they know actively, using methods of their choice to demonstrate competency. A third pillar is Multiple Means of Engagement, which promotes the idea that because students are interested in different things, if only one method is used to try to capture and maintain their attention, there will inevitably be others who are disengaged. Educators, therefore, should attempt to engage students in a multitude of ways.

This book isn't meant to be a road map for how to implement the principles of Universal Design for Learning. Instead, the purpose is to examine how UDL converges with other contemporary educational philosophies to bring about a positive change for all students, including those with disabilities (see Figure 2.1).

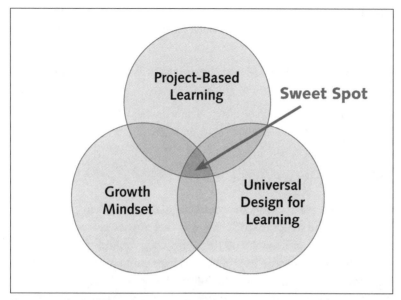

Figure 2.1 The sweet spot between Universal Design for Learning, Project-Based Learning, and Growth Mindset.

The Impact of Shifting Guidelines

The concept of Universal Design for Learning has been ~~ar~~ ~~ ~~ for a long time, but it has often been misrepresented or misinterpreted as a ~~ ~~~~ive exclusively for students with disabilities, or as something under the purvue of those working only in special education. However, federal guidelines have helped issue forth change to the perception of UDL, facilitating adoption and implementation by everyone.

The National Education Technology Plans of 2010 and 2016

In November of 2010, the United States Department of Education published a National Education Technology Plan (bit.ly/usnetp2010). The model described in the plan calls for engaging and empowering personalized learning experiences for every learner. The introductory statement calls for the use of "state-of-the-art technology and Universal Design for Learning (UDL) concepts to enable, motivate, and inspire all students to achieve, regardless of background, languages, or disabilities." The concepts of the Open Learning Initiative (OLI), accessible educational materials, and the use of contemporary technologies are all also woven into the document.

In 2016, an updated National Education Technology Plan, titled *Future Ready Learning: Reimagining the Role of Technology in Education*, was published, placing equity and accessibility in the forefront (bit.ly/usnetp16). The document and accompanying website offer guidance, resources, and examples for the successful implementation of Universal Design for Learning to prepare students for an unpredictable future. The updated plan includes a call for implementation of strategies to facilitate a Growth Mindset, increase learner agency by empowering choice-making through universal design, solving authentic problems, and enabling technologies to break down long-standing cultural barriers.

As the principle document outlining a national philosophy on the implementation of technology in education, this plan highlights the notion that educational experiences should be designed with everyone in mind. Those striving to embrace UDL practices throughout their educational agency can point to this document as evidence to embrace these principles as a foundation upon which to build the future.

Every Student Succeeds Act of 2015

In 2015 in the United States, the Every Student Succeeds Act (Public Law 114-95) was signed (www.ed.gov/essa) reauthorizing and updating the Elementary and Secondary Education Act (ESEA) signed into law in 1965. The law requires that each state shall develop a plan "to demonstrate that the state educational agency, in consultation with local educational agencies, has implemented a set of high-quality student academic assessments in mathematics, reading or language arts, and science," in addition to "the appropriate accommodations such as interoperability with and ability to use assistive technology for children with disabilities, including students with the most significant cognitive disabilities, and students with a disability who are provided accommodations under an act other than the Individuals with Disabilities Education Act, necessary to measure the academic achievement of such children relative to the challenging state academic standards or alternate academic achievement standards," and "be developed, to the extent practicable, using the principles of Universal Design for Learning."

It also requires that "states that receive allotments from the federal government shall increase access to personalized, rigorous learning experiences supported by technology by identifying and addressing technology-readiness needs, including computer devices, access to school libraries, internet connectivity, operating systems, software, related network infrastructure, and data security; using technology, consistent with the principles of Universal Design for Learning, to support the learning needs of all students, including children with disabilities and English learners."

The law directly ties funding to the development of an action plan that uses UDL as a framework for increasing access to technology to address the needs of all students, including those with disabilities. What once was a choice to adopt the principles of UDL has become an expectation.

Empowerment Before Engagement

One of the three principles of Universal Design for Learning is to create experiences in which students are engaged using multiple means. Engagement, however, doesn't necessarily promote active involvement or ownership over the learning. Consider the example of going to a theater to watch a magician. While in your seat and watching the hocus-pocus, seeing the wizard disappear or saw someone in half, you might be completely engaged. The experience of being at a magic show, however, is passive. As much as you are into the tricks, the act, and the atmosphere of the entire experience, you aren't necessarily empowered by it. Most audience members don't leave a magic show wanting to become the next Harry Houdini.

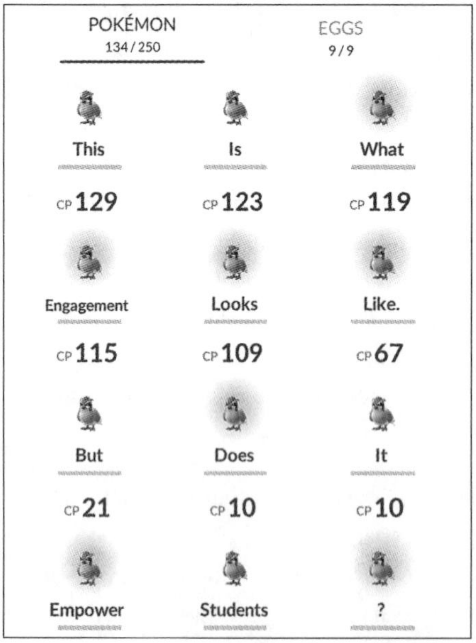

Figure 2.2 Pokémon Go is a lot of fun to play— it is very engaging! But is it also empowering?

In contrast, consider when you're participating in an activity related to a topic of high interest to you. Perhaps you've seen a problem in the world and have felt the need to do something about it. You have been given the power to use whatever tools you choose to act upon your desire. Creating, making, and doing something that makes a point or a difference by educating or otherwise engaging others is truly empowering. Participation spawned by internal motivations to do and learn more is what drives curiosity and promotes active learning. When empowered, not just engaged, students are willing, active participants who take ownership and responsibility for their own learning (see Figure 2.2).

Bring Your Own Technology

How many different devices do you use throughout the day? Do you have a smartphone? A tablet? A laptop? An internet-browser-only device? Do you use a device where the primary user interface is voice commands? Are you wearing any technology right now? As adults, technology has become part of our daily operations, carried with us ubiquitously or readily accessible in our environment. Why should school or the classroom be any different?

The technology we choose for any given task is determined by what would be the most efficient or comfortable based on what we are trying to accomplish. Sometimes it is best to use a phone; other times, it is best to use a computer with a full-size keyboard. Sometimes a tablet is needed. The more opportunities one has to make these choices, the more practice that person has at selecting the right tool—and the better they become at using it.

Tool selection is a skill that can be explicitly taught in context with the task the student is attempting. Ideally, students choose what works best for them and develop a comfort level with specific pieces of technology. Although functionalities might be similar across devices, how a person accesses those functions through the user interface may be vastly different. For instance, on one device, the ability to have text on the screen read aloud might be engaged by swiping down on the screen with two fingers. On another device, one might need to launch an application to enable this feature. The function may exist in both places, but locating it on a device with which you are unfamiliar can take precious time and energy when what you're really attempting to do is complete a different task or solve a different problem.

Technology is most effective when it works seamlessly in the background, becoming effortless for the user over time. Once one is familiar with a piece of technology, being forced to use a different piece of technology with similar capabilities (for example, something provided by the school when a personal device performs the same function) can be frustrating. Imagine practicing baseball for years and having a very limited knowledge of golf. Then one day, someone takes you to a golf course, hands you a golf club, and expects you to make par with it, telling you that golf is similar to baseball because in both sports people hit balls with sticks.

Technology becomes personalized and customized the more you use it. Although a person might be capable of learning how to use a new piece of technology, expecting this person to be as efficient or effective using that unfamiliar technology is unrealistic. Educational experience designers understand that one way to make the experience positive is to encourage people to make their own choices about the technology they try, use, and adopt whenever possible. This helps ensure the technology becomes integrated into what a person does and who they are, and corresponds with who they want to be.

When a person brings his or her own device into an experience where he or she can use it to learn, a level of comfort already exists. Less time needs to be spent learning how to operate the technology and more time can be spent on engaging in the experience with the technology of choice.

Choosing one's own device is important for any learner but particularly so for students with disabilities. Depending on the disability, it might take longer to cognitively or physically learn how to access a new function. For instance, if a person with a disability has learned the motor pattern for accessing a text-to-speech function on a particular device, changing that device might mean changing that motor pattern that the individual has come to rely upon. To the greatest extent possible, allow students to utilize the devices with which they are most accustomed. When not possible, understand and expect that learning to use unfamiliar technology when already familiar with a different piece of technology takes time, effort, and understanding.

A TOOLS CHECKLIST

One strategy to help a student practice and learn the skill of selecting the appropriate tool for an educational experience is to help that student generate a list of tools accessible to him or her in the environment (Figure 2.3). The educational experience designer doesn't do this *for* the student but, instead, works on this *with* the student.

The student can start by asking the question "What can I use to get this job done?" and then generate a list of available tools. The educational experience designer acts as guide by providing the student with prompts and reminders of the technology at his or her disposal while generating the list. Additionally, the student could list some pros and cons or strengths and weaknesses of each tool. These characteristics could then be referenced when the student is asked to make a choice about which tool is most appropriate. The educational experience designer assists the student in his or her selection by asking guiding questions about the tools, the individual, and the task at hand: "Why are you selecting this tool? What aspects of this tool do you prefer over another tool? Has this tool worked for you in past educational experiences?"

It is important to realize that the educational experience designer

---

Tools Checklist

Complete this checklist to help you reflect on which tool to use for the activity.

* Required

What is the activity?
Choose ▼

For which subject/class is this activity?
Choose ▼

Which tool(s) should I use to complete this activity? *
☐ Writing on paper with a pen or pencil
☐ Screencast on tablet
☐ Writing on paper with a marker
☐ Word processing on laptop
☐ Voice recording on tablet
☐ Comic-strip generator
☐ Screencast on laptop
☐ Voice recording on laptop
☐ Editing checklist
☐ Writing on dry-erase board
☐ Word prediction
☐ Word processing on tablet
☐ Speech recognition
☐ Writing on a slant board
☐ Word cloud generator
☐ Other: _____

How useful would you rate the tools you used when the activity was completed?

	0	1	2	3	4	5	
Not useful	○	○	○	○	○	○	Really useful

Reflect (Optional): What are your thoughts about the tool you selected for the activity? What worked? What would you do differently?
Your answer

[SUBMIT]   ▬▬▬▬▬▬ Page 1 of 1

Never submit passwords through Google Forms.

Figure 2.3 Sample tools checklist using a Google form (bit.ly/sampletoolschecklist).

does not select the tool for the student unless working in conjunction with the Individualized Education Program team to support a student who cannot yet maintain the physical, cognitive, or developmental ability to do so on his or her own. The educational experience designer does not prevent the student from making a selection even if it is not the best option. It is the responsibility of the educational experience designer to assist the student in reflecting on the choice of technology before, during, and at the end of the task. This self-reflection will help the student learn how to make appropriate choices in the future and, ultimately, on their own.

Project-Based Learning

Here's the problem: Our world will always have a large quantity of problems to solve. So, how do we solve *that* problem? Answer: educational institutions can become the breeding ground for imaginative solutions.

The idea behind a Project-Based Learning (PBL) approach is that education should be about investigating the solutions to real-world problems. An educator starts by introducing an authentic problem that is impacting either an individual or the local, regional, or global community. The educator's job is to introduce the problem to students who will then become invested in attempting to solve it. From there, the students investigate the problem by doing research, gathering facts and other evidence to understand the underlying factors causing the problem. Next, the students collaborate to generate a plan (or plans) of action to address the problem, and then they execute that plan.

The students lead the charge and drive the change they want to see, sharing their solutions with the wider world. Educators act as guides along the journey, offering insights on how to manage and organize the students' endeavors. The role of the educator is to assist the students in locating, selecting, and acquiring the tools and resources they need to complete the project that addresses the given problem. Along the way, students experience the content and meet the same instructional standards they would have encountered had the instruction been educator led. Using the PBL approach, students become empowered, engaged, and invested in the learning. They authentically practice becoming critical thinkers and problem solvers. Every student, using his or her differing talents and abilities, learns that individual contributions to the work matter and have a positive impact.

Which Problem Do You Want to Solve?

Human brains are wired to answer questions—it's why we love a good mystery, riddle, or brain teaser. Few things in life are as gratifying as discovering a solution to a problem. Project-Based Learning starts by outlining something that needs fixing. Students then put their minds and bodies to work trying to address that problem, learning and practicing the skills of collaboration, communication, critical thinking, and evidence-based research along the way.

As educators (or really, *any* adult interacting with a student from an early age), the question to ask students is not what they want to be when they get older but "Which problems do you want to work to solve?" The ever-changing future might not have the need for the job they currently seek. Designing educational experiences that invite students, with or without disabilities, to become problem solvers rather than occupation seekers prepares them with the tools, skills, and mindset that no matter what the future has in store, they'll be able to approach it, tackle it, handle it, deal with it, and ultimately, solve it. The world will never have a shortage of problems to solve.

Students Helping Students

One authentic scenario that will need to be addressed continuously in every school is the creation and implementation of tools and resources to help people with varying abilities. Get students invested in the idea that there are other students, friends, or potential friends who have a different set of challenges when attempting to engage, participate, problem solve, and learn alongside their peers.

Presenting students with these barriers might inspire them to want to pick up a sledgehammer to break through them. Point out which problems are occurring with students with disabilities right at your very own school, and invite all of your students to work to solve them. When students apply themselves to empowering others in their immediate community, the culture of education shifts toward the positive to the benefit of everybody.

What follows are examples of problems that have either been or are currently being solved by students.

Communication-Partner Training Materials

Some students are helping each other learn language using an augmentative/alternative communication (AAC) device. Due to the visual nature, vocabulary, and structure of many AAC systems, learning language using an AAC device can help students practice new vocabulary and sight words while learning the structure or syntax of language. In some schools, upper elementary students who travel down to the kindergarten classrooms to participate in a reading-buddy program might also create materials to support the educational lessons of the students learning to use the AAC devices (Figure 2.4).

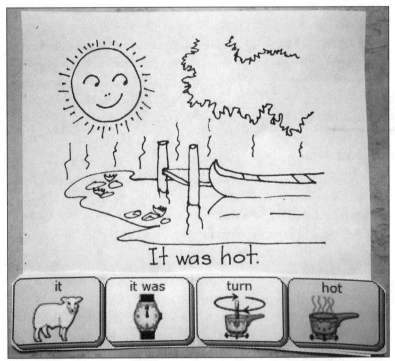

Figure 2.4 Page of a book adapted with augmentative/alternative communication (AAC) icons used by communication partners when modeling language.

CONNECTED

In 2013, President Obama announced an initiative called ConnectED, which was designed to empower educators to implement technology and to supply them with the professional development to learn how to use it (tech.ed.gov/connected). The initiative also took aim at individualized learning by empowering students through digital content.

The main purpose of the initiative was to prepare students with the skills and abilities necessary to compete for jobs globally. One of the initiative's goals was to provide the infrastructure necessary to supply 99 percent of students with access to high-speed broadband by 2018. The increase in connectivity was meant to transform the learning experience within a school setting for every student, regardless of disability or income. The ConnectED initiative is an example of how educational leaders in America have placed the contemporary focus of education improvement squarely on the back of interactive, personalized learning experiences that use connected technologies.

Simplified Materials for Complex Topics

Some students might have a strong interest in a subject but have trouble locating understandable materials presented in different formats or at a reading level that would empower them to access text. As a potential way for others to demonstrate what they've learned about a complex topic, students can create accessible, digital books with simplified text. These books can then be shared with students who need the material presented to them differently. The Tar Heel Reader site (tarheelreader.org) is one example of a user-created, accessible library of books that students author and publish, providing searchable content for other users. And books are only one media format that could be created. Videos, audio files, comic strips, multimedia slideshow presentations, and interactive tabletop or digital games are additional options.

For example, high school teachers in a team-taught English class explained to their students that elementary-aged students were learning concepts related to Egypt, animal habitats, and addition with regrouping. Since the high school students were learning how to write detailed instructions, the teachers invited the high schoolers to attempt to teach the elementary students the three topics by creating interactive materials of their own choice. The high school students innovated to create multiple materials, including switch-activated multimedia slideshows, card games, and tabletop games. The high school students demonstrated understanding and proficiency in specific areas of writing while producing work that authentically helped the elementary students better understand and engage with the content they were learning.

Captioning Existing Video

YouTube continues to be a primary source for finding both educational and entertaining video content. However, many of the videos are not captioned, or do not maintain subtitles in English or other languages. Students can practice keyboarding skills by transcribing a video. The transcriptions can then be sent to the creator of the video for inclusion in the description, time coded and posted as an actual caption/subtitle, or simply be posted in the comments by the transcriber. YouTube also allows channel managers to activate a crowdsource captioning feature on individual videos or throughout an entire channel. Having students caption video helps to solve accessibility problems, reinforces positive digital citizenship, and promotes a culture of inclusion.

The Maker Movement

Let's get together and make stuff—that's the underlying principle behind the maker movement. Perhaps the most popular versions of maker clubs are made up of those who tinker with electronic gadgets. Most makerspaces are filled with soldering irons, circuits, wires, and healthy amounts of duct tape, and topped off by a 3-D printer. However, maker clubs or fairs are not limited to those who like gizmos. They can just as easily be built around baking, sewing, or any other craft that involves solving a problem and creating a product. Although commonly associated with the creation of something tangible, the final product might also be something digital, such as a video, an audio product, or something graphical in nature.

With this in mind, makerspaces and the people involved in them can use their talents to create materials to assist students with disabilities. Instead of just tinkering, makers can be presented with an authentic accessibility challenge, work together to brainstorm a way to address the situation, and then create a potential solution. Projects focused on increased accessibility include making adaptations to technology, perhaps adding switches to drive rideable toys or battery-operated toys, building holders for tablets and phones, or creating accessible games and books (see Figure 2.5).

Figure 2.5 Students from the Assistive Technology Maker Club at Harmony Middle School in Hamilton, Virginia, adapt ride-on toys, games, and other items to make them more accessible.

Whether making an official makerspace or just adopting this mentality during lesson design, educators can create an environment that embodies the philosophy that no matter who you are and what skills you have, it's rewarding and fun to bring something new into the world. What makes the experience even more rewarding is if the thing you are creating helps to solve a problem, such as helping someone access text, move around their environment, play with their peers, or communicate with others. For example, a preschool student was having difficulty accessing a communication device. When the device was first presented to him, he attempted to press the cells with the thumb on his right hand. His fingers would accidentally touch the screen, activating a word he didn't intend. Presented with the problem, student makers created a stand to move the surface from a horizontal plane to a vertical plane. Once upright, the student began using his forefinger to activate the cells, eliminating mishits.

At the heart of the maker movement is the notion that anyone and everyone is driven to use their imagination to create. Educators can leverage this innate drive in students, harness that spirit, and focus it into learning experiences. Instead of designing activities with the consumption of content at the core of the lesson, the experience can be designed around the creation of a product that helps others, whether it be tangible or digital. When one is driven and challenged to use any means at their disposal to make something, learning takes place.

Growth Mindset

Do you believe that there are some problems that you just won't be able to solve? Or do you believe that given enough time, you can solve any problem set before you?

In Dr. Carol Dweck's book *Mindset*, she describes two different types of people (Dweck, 2017). Some people approach a task with the belief that they either have the skills to complete the task or they don't. She calls this approach the "Fixed Mindset." Other people approach a task or challenge with a "Growth Mindset"—a belief that if they do not know how to complete the task that, given enough time, energy, and effort, they can and will learn how.

Which type of person are you? Which type of person do you want to be? Which type of person do you want your students to be?

The experiences we design and the language we use when addressing students can foster and formulate a particular mindset. A task where students are asked to determine either a right or wrong answer, like many tests given in traditional classrooms, fosters a Fixed Mindset. Think of most traditional examinations or tests you have taken: the majority of questions asked have had exactly one answer, and you, as the individual taking the test, can either get it right or wrong. You either know it or you don't.

Tackling a problem where the answer is uncertain at the onset changes the dynamic completely. Instead, what is being assessed isn't one's ability to get to a predetermined solution but how one approaches the problem, which resources the person uses to attack the challenge, and the determination one shows in finding a potential solution.

Facilitating a Growth Mindset is critical for all students but especially for those with disabilities. When the learning experience is designed with open-ended solutions as possibilities, the student can attack the problem utilizing his or her abilities—no matter what they are—with confidence. Then, when faced with any future problem, the student will approach it with the same belief that somehow, some way, he or she can figure out how to solve it.

For example, learning to decode text is a skill taught in the primary grades. A student with a disability that impacts her ability to decode might quickly adopt the idea that reading is a difficult task for her. She might even say to herself, "I'm not a good reader," branding her psyche with the notion that reading will always be a challenge for her and carrying that weight around into future versions of herself. The attitudes and words used by the adults meant to support her have an impact. Educators attempting to facilitate a Growth Mindset within the student might provide support by conveying messages such as, "You're practicing your phonics. You haven't mastered some sounds yet, but as we continue to work at it, you'll continue to see yourself get better and better at it." Consistent feedback using language that demonstrates the progress being made helps the student realize that there are not two camps of people—those who are good at reading and those who are not. Instead, she'll develop a mindset that with time, effort, and determination, she'll keep getting better at the skill of decoding and emerge as a competent reader.

AWESOME INSIGHT

Learners are independent of one another. The act of learning is an intensely personal experience infused with a person's sense of being, worth, and personality. The time it takes to learn any given skill is unique to the individual and is not dependent on anyone else's experience. Some students might take five minutes to understand a concept while another might take five hours. In both instances, both students are learning.

Do you think you can foster a Growth Mindset in yourself and the students with whom you work? Is it possible? Will you give up or will you utilize resources to figure it out? Will you call a friend? Post a question on an online community? Do an internet search? Ask Alexa, Cortana, Siri, or Google? Will you give up? Or will you foster the belief that someday, given enough time, you'll figure it out and always continue to improve?

Standards-Based Grading and Portfolios

What is the purpose of providing a grade to a student? What do grades really mean? What if there were no grades? Instead, what if there were only the obligation to provide evidence that learning has taken place? Standards-based grading is an approach to assessment that suggests learning can be measured by presenting evidence related to the standard as opposed to presenting students with a test and assigning a percentage or a grade. Students work at their own pace to achieve standard after standard, demonstrating competency of each by presenting evidence to support the claim that they understand the content. Regardless of ability, students demonstrate progress toward the learning objective.

Students, so passionate about the content they are learning, keep track of their own progress toward the achievement of their own goals. They report to the educational experience designer what they've learned along with the demonstration of a level of mastery or competency over a piece of content or skill. The student's reflection on the process provides all the evidence necessary that learning is taking place. Documentation of this evidence collected by both the students and the educational experience designers is reported using portfolios, which grow with each student over time. Grades need not be comparative, competitive, compulsory, or catastrophic. Instead, the report can be a truly reflective measure of how a student perceives how his or her own learning is progressing.

Mr. Tyson Loses Lectures

As a former high school earth science and chemistry teacher turned educational experience designer for earth science and chemistry in high school, Mr. Tyson made a shift. For years, he stood in front of the classroom and lectured to students for a large portion of his class, attempting to captivate them with his charm and wit. He used jokes like "I don't trust atoms—they make up everything"; "All the good chemistry jokes argon"; and "I was going to have a party in space, but I wasn't sure how to planet." Despite his sense of humor and colorful multimedia slideshows, he felt frustrated because a growing number of students seemed disinterested.

He tried to think of different methods to present the content in engaging ways, but the students weren't responding. A small percentage of his students, like those who were learning English as a second language or the students with disabilities, through no fault of their own, found it difficult to understand the material. Mr. Tyson was relieved they had the support of a team teacher present to re-explain things in a different way. Despite the captive audience, he could tell his song and dance just wasn't working to build the passion and love for science he wished for his students. At first, he blamed the students, thinking them lazy, tardy, absent, and distracted, even when physically present. Smartphones and other portable devices were no help. Today's generation just wanted to be texting and scrolling through their social media feeds rather than learning about Sir Isaac Newton and Carl Sagan. Mr. Tyson also blamed middle school teachers who didn't know how to do their jobs, parents who would rather be friends with their kids than parents, and an entire generation that had gone soft, not wanting to put in the hard work necessary to achieve success.

Not only did he see it this way, but many of his colleagues were seeing the same thing too (and saying as much in the staff lounge). For a while, he had convinced himself that this was just how things were—an unfortunate reality. What hope did he have in changing an entire generation? He decided to stop working so hard in the development of new materials. After all, with the deck stacked so heavily against him, what chance would he have in changing the work habits of his students?

But Mr. Tyson did not like to think of himself as a person who phoned in his work. He did not want to resign himself to a daily grind of malaise and misery. He would be no better than all those he blamed for his dissatisfaction if he couldn't make a change.

So, Mr. Tyson made one of the most difficult choices of his life. Instead of focusing on the actions of others, he asked himself one very tough and poignant question: "What can I do to make the change I'd like to see happen for my students?" It was a question he wasn't sure he knew how to answer, but being the scientist he was, he began to research the problem.

Looking back, he can't pinpoint one precise moment, event, or occurrence that provided the catalyst for his change in perception. He never shrieked "Eureka!" or yelled "By George, I think I've got it!" Perhaps it was a combination of videos he watched, conversations on social media with other educators who had varying views, supportive questions sparked through professional-development sessions organized by his administration, podcasts he listened to on his way to school, and a book he started reading published by ISTE. And Mr. Tyson's epiphany did not come all at once in a thunderous wave but, rather, in a slow, steady rising of the tide. Without knowing exactly how or why, Mr. Tyson underwent the transformation from teacher to educational experience designer.

Mr. Tyson, with a new concept for what education could be in his mind, made some changes. First, he ditched the lectures. He made himself a rule that he would talk to the whole group for no longer than five minutes at a time. His goal was to turn the ratio of time *he* spent talking to time *the students* spent talking on its head. Instead of focusing on delivering a piece of content on a given topic, he focused on capitalizing on the spirit of sensibility and sensitivity that seemed to reside inherently in most of his students. He would tap into his students' innate sense of wonder and curiosity, and the brain's need to solve problems.

He presented the students with authentic problems facing the local and global communities, and even some in the school that were impacting the student's day-to-day lives. He then invited the students to communicate and work together but gave them the flexibility to work collaboratively or independently. Mr. Tyson guided students to different resources available, including hardware—like their personal devices or school laptops, software on the computers, and other online applications. Recognizing that movement was an integral part of success, he encouraged students to get up and move around while working. Some students sat in groups clustered around a laptop screen while others stood around a lab table, typing information on tablets.

Mr. Tyson glided from group to group, asking guiding questions rather than providing answers. Occasionally, when the moment called for it, he activated an alarm (one that flashed and buzzed) on his own phone, signaling the need for a few moments of whole-class attention in which he'd clarify a point, highlight a discovery, spotlight a technique being used, or offer a quick demonstration. The students learning English as a second language and the students with disabilities worked in conjunction with peers, capitalizing on their strengths and choosing their preferred method of participation. Mr. Tyson challenged the students to not only research the problem but do something about it.

Inspired, empowered, and armed with knowledge, day after day, inside of class and out, students worked on methods for solving the problems. He found some students hooked and listening to science podcasts. Other students voluntarily read books (which, in the past, he might have assigned); and overall, students arrived to class with questions they had been pondering, artifacts and resources they had discovered, and materials they had created. Mr. Tyson found students were falling in love with learning about science.

Mr. Tyson also discovered that he was more satisfied and reinvigorated too—he wanted to go to work. Every day wasn't perfect, but the experience was challenging and ultimately rewarding. Due to his shift in perception and action, students found themselves inspired to solve problems using the science he was trained to teach them. And his efforts weren't just helping the students learn science but making a positive difference in the world.

LET THEM GO

The screen glows white on the computing device—
not a worksheet to be seen.
A culture of innovation,
and I wonder where it's been.

Each kid is yelling that the learning "is mine!"
All want to sign in.
Everyone has tried…

Don't let them in.
Don't let them see.
Change the password—what should it be?
Surreal—so unreal—
everyone should grow.
There's so much to know…

Let them go! Let them go!
Don't hold 'em back anymore.

Let them go! Let them go!
Plan today to give them more.

They don't care,
when you talk all day.
Let the change rage on.
They want to make something every day!

It's funny how some tools
make the world seem so small.
And the wires that once connected me
don't tangle them at all.

It's time to see what they can do.
No tests, no limits to break through.
Their right, not wrong. For them, not me.
They're free!

Let them go! Let them go!
They make mistakes, but at least they tried.
Let them go! Let them go!
School never makes them cry.

Here they learn
and here they play!
Let the change rage on!

Your power hurries as you break through to new ground.
Your plans are growing into brazen actions all around.
And one thought materializes, but it's an awesome task.
You're never going back. The past is in the past!

Let them go! Let them go!
And they'll break out into song!
Let them go! Let them go!
Perfect students begone.

Here they stand!
They learn each day!
Let the change rage on!
They want to make something every day!

CHAPTER 3

Considerations for Students with Disabilities

Educational experience designers demonstrate a professional set of characteristics to foster and create a learning environment that works for everyone. They work to develop inclusive and accessible practices for every experience they design. They design lessons for everyone rather than retrofit for a few. This chapter is a guide for how to adopt practices and design experiences that promote learning for everyone but especially for students with disabilities.

In this chapter, you'll:

1. Explore how the language we use and the presumptions we make about students with disabilities impact their educational experiences.

2. Examine a philosophy for the selection and implementation of accessible materials.

ISTE STANDARDS ADDRESSED

ISTE Standards for Educators 2a. Shape, advance, and accelerate a shared vision for empowered learning with technology by engaging with education stakeholders.

ISTE Standards for Educators 2b. Advocate for equitable access to educational technology, digital content, and learning opportunities to meet the diverse needs of all students.

ISTE Standards for Educators 2c. Model for colleagues the identification, exploration, evaluation, curation, and adoption of new digital resources and tools for learning.

ISTE Standards for Educators 3b. Establish a learning culture that promotes curiosity and critical examination of online resources and fosters digital literacy and media fluency.

ISTE Standards for Educators 5c. Explore and apply instructional design principles to create innovative digital learning environments that engage and support learning.

ISTE Standards for Educators 6b. Manage the use of technology and student learning strategies in digital platforms, virtual environments, hands-on makerspaces, and/or in the field.

The Least Dangerous Assumption

When you are meeting a person for the first time, or when you are working with an individual and you don't know that person's abilities, what are some reasonable assumptions to make? When faced with the unknown, what expectations should you have of another person?

In a study of how our expectations impact others (Rosenthal & Fode, 1963), researchers placed labels on two sets of standard albino lab rats that were about to enter the same maze. One set of rats was labeled "maze bright," indicating they were genetically bred to be good at mazes, and the other set of rats was labeled "maze dull," with no particular talents toward completing mazes. The researchers then invited people to observe the activity of the rats running through the maze. With all other variables consistent except for the labels, the researchers found that the rats surrounded by people who believed them to be better at the task outperformed those who were labeled as not being bred for the task, learning more quickly how to navigate the maze.

A version of the experiment was repeated with students and educators. At the beginning of a school year, students in a specific school were given an IQ test. Teachers were told that, based on the results, a number of students were ready to academically "bloom." In actuality, the IQ test given had no predictive value, and there was no known difference between students labeled or not labeled. At the end of the year, the test was readministered, and those students who had been identified as academic bloomers outperformed those who were not labeled (Rosenthal & Jacobson, 1963). The study suggests that when people hold high expectations and positive assumptions about others, those people do better; our presumptions can have an impact on the performance of others. Therefore, when the abilities of a person with whom we are working are unknown, it is best to assume that the person is competent. To ensure optimal performance, it is necessary to hold high—if not limitless—expectations.

Underestimating a person's abilities and potential to gain additional abilities can be catastrophic to that individual's performance, self-worth, and entire future. When you don't know, err on the side of believing in people. It is better to be wrong about someone's abilities than to assume that person doesn't have or will never obtain those abilities.

Educational experience designers never stop believing that, one day, once we figure out how best to teach each student, every student has the ability to learn.

When conclusive data is absent, educational decisions should be based on assumptions that, if incorrect, will be the least dangerous—the least likely to have a negative impact on that individual's ability to function independently as an adult (Donnellan, 1984). The article also suggested that it is less dangerous to an individual to assume that poor performance is due to the inadequacy of the instruction rather than a lack of ability on the part the individual. When a student is struggling to meet educational goals, those supporting that individual should question the design of the instruction, not the abilities of the individual.

An expansion on these principles can be used to shift the culture of how people approach assisting a person with a disability to achieve educational goals (Jorgensen, 2005). These principles include the understanding that everyone has different talents and skills, intelligence is not one-dimensional, and a person's future educational path cannot be dictated by attempting to measure intelligence alone. It suggests that people learn best when they are perceived as having value, with the expectation of success.

These findings indicate that unless you have proof otherwise, presume everyone, regardless of an identified disability, is competent. Everyone has different abilities, but one of the fundamental principles behind education is the idea that everyone can use those abilities to gain more abilities. In this way, every person can move forward on a path to achieving whatever goal they set.

This journey is what brings about positive change in the world, and everyone has a part to play. This includes people with disabilities, no matter the type or severity. When you meet a new person, you make certain assumptions. You expect the person to have understood whatever the message was when you started the interaction. You expect that if you address that person, he or she will acknowledge your presence, and you will likely expect that the individual will respond in some way. There might even be more subtle expectations as well, depending on the environment you're in, like expecting someone to greet you when you come into a room or say farewell when leaving. One only ceases to have these expectations when evidence is provided that contradicts these social structures. When interacting with a person with a disability, the expectation should be the same.

When designing educational experiences, lead with the assumption that students will have the ability to participate in the lesson. Give students the opportunity to fail by trying. Be surprised when a student fails, not when he or she succeeds. Construct learning opportunities without limits. Students often jump only as high as the bar you set, so the inherent risk to setting a bar is not setting it high enough. Rather than guessing at where to set the bar, don't set a bar at all.

THE RIDDLE OF THE SPHINX

The brave knight stood before the sphinx—this was his final trial. Answer correctly, and he would complete his quest, saving himself, the kingdom, and all within it. Fail, and… Well, he best not contemplate failure. The ground was littered with the remnants of those who had not succeeded. This game was a matter of life and death.

The knight took a moment to bolster his confidence and nodded, accepting the challenge. Raspy voices of millions of children exploded in his head.

Learning begins
at birth or before.
Every person
goes through the door.

Some go fast.
Some go slow.
We all move
at our own tempo.

Sometimes it stops.
Sometimes it breaks.
No one can help
but make some mistakes.

Who is at fault?
Who is to blame?
The answer is always,
always the same.

Whoever it is,
this person's it's not.
But with that said,
it happens a lot.

Who should it be—
the one that we shame?
The one who has failed
this learning game.

Is it the pupil—
the one who has lost?
Or maybe the teacher
should be the one tossed?

What do you say,
knight of the king?
Insight and wisdom
is what you do bring.

The fault lies with one—
what do you say?
Student or teacher?
Show me the way.

Give me your answer.
Tell me what's true.
Who is at fault
when learning falls through?

The childrens' voices fell silent in his mind.

The knight removed his helmet and placed it on the ground beside him. He then removed his metal gloves, letting them drop to the sand. His fingers massaged his chin, and he began to pace.

"Let me think…" he began.

"You speak of students, teachers, and learning that has failed. Let's start with the assumption that it is never, ever the student's fault. If that is true, then it must be the teacher's fault. However, even the most skilled, well-equipped, well-trained knight can lose a battle. Teachers, like knights in a fight, might try everything in their power and beyond to invigorate the spirit of learning in a youth. Those who are not accepting of assistance make it difficult to assist them. Therefore, the fault may not be with the teacher either.

"If it isn't the student and it isn't the teacher, well, then it must be…

"Sphinx, I have my answer."

A heavy silence descended over the plain. Anticipation was a starving creature clamoring to be fed.

"The answer is no one. No one is to blame. It is no one's fault when learning subsides. If fault needs to lie with something, it is with a system that allows such failure to exist in the first place. This fault, however, lies with no singular person. The answer to your riddle is the system. It is the system that needs to change."

The sphinx's great head nodded as the voices rang out.

"You may pass."

AWESOME INSIGHT

When brainstorming strategies for how to help educate a student, start with the premise that no matter the circumstances, there is no one to blame. Presume the student is not at fault. Presume the educators are not at fault. Presume the parents are not at fault. If you need someone to blame, blame the system, and move forward with trying to fix it. Expect success, and if there is ever a struggle to meet goals, provide assistance without blame.

The "Able To" Challenge

When you began reading this book, were you able to open it or did you just open it? When you made your last warm meal, were you able to cook it or did you just cook it? When you last felt enjoyment, were you able to smile or did you just smile? These might seem like redundant questions—of course, you likely just opened the book, cooked the meal, and smiled a smile. By extension, you were *able* to do all three, but the way we phrase our communication impacts public perceptions and provides subtle shifts in our cultural mindset. The language we use matters.

Over time, there are certain words or phrases that were once commonplace that have now been ostracized because of their derogatory nature. I'm certain you can think of a few, and just thinking of them makes you feel awkward. An example of a term like this is the word *retarded* when used to describe a person. Currently and continuously, there's a movement to ban the use of the word to describe a person or an action. Once used both colloquially and professionally, it is now generally thought of as hurtful and degrading. Using it shows an overall lack of respect for fellow humans.

There is another, more subtle but just as insidious commonly used phrase that permeates educational writings, assessment and evaluation reports, Individualized Education Program documents, progress reports, and spoken language that also degrades the individual of whom we are reporting (see Figure 3.1). Are you *able* to deduce it? Are you *able* to figure it out? Are you *able* to be ready for the phrase to be revealed?

Figure 3.1 Is this woman *wearing the shirt* or is she *able to wear the shirt*? What is the difference between these two phrases?

Imagine using "able to" to describe all the things you do in a day. Do they sound redundant? Does it change the overt or the implied meaning (see Table 3.1)?

"Able to" is also used to communicate genuine surprise that an action could actually be accomplished because of the great effort involved. For example, saying "I ran a marathon" implies a different meaning than saying "I was able to run a marathon." Likewise, "I jumped out of a plane" makes it sound like this action was something easy to do. "I was able to jump out of a plane" makes it sound like you were hesitant, skittish, and using tremendous amounts of willpower to perform such a daring feat. It might also sound like something was in your way, impeding your exit, but somehow, you found a way to overcome that barrier.

"Able to" can also be used in reference to obtaining permission. "I was able to go out with my friends tonight" or "I was able to get dad's car for the night" implies that an authority figure was asked and granted permission, as opposed to "I went out with my friends tonight" or "I got my dad's car for the night."

Table 3.1 A Look at "Able To" Statements

Adding "Able To" to Tasks	Analysis of Implied Meaning
I am able to walk to school.	Does that mean I live close to the school or that I can physically walk there? How does it change when I say, *I walk to school?*
I am able to put on pants.	Does this imply some difficulty or effort as opposed to *I put on my pants?*
I am able to forgive you.	This phrasing implies a struggle; *I forgive you* doesn't.
I am able to love my mom.	This sentence makes your mom sound like a really awful person, but you choose to love her anyway because she's your mom. The meaning changes dramatically when you simply state, *I love my mom.*

In an education context, evaluation reports, levels of academic and functional performance within Individualized Education Programs, and progress notes top the list of items containing written exposition describing the abilities of an individual. In those narratives, the phrase "able to" is used repeatedly to describe a student's performance. Here are some actual examples from educational reports and Individualized Education Programs (only with the names changed):

"Tucker was able to activate the cell" versus "Tucker activated the cell."

"Maggie is able to write five-paragraph essays" versus "Maggie writes five-paragraph essays."

"Melissa is able to say 10 words verbally" versus "Melissa says 10 words verbally."

Reading and writing "able to" regarding a person's ability implies that the author is genuinely surprised that the subject is capable of doing the action in the sentence. It screams, "I didn't expect that person was capable of doing that action, but he did it!" Or it implies that some tremendous effort was required to accomplish the task.

Instead of being surprised by achievement, performance, or accomplishment, educational experience designers assume and expect it. Presume that the student is competent in any task until he or she proves otherwise, and use words that reflect this presumption. Words shape our culture and influence public perception. Challenge yourself to craft sentences without the phrase "able to" to eliminate the unearthly effort inherent to the phrase. Are you able to do it?

People, Not Puzzles

Sometime in your past, you might have heard someone say that she or he wanted to work with people with disabilities because they wanted to figure out what's going on with them. They might have explained that they want to help the person by pouring through the evaluation data to figure out what makes the person tick. They might have drawn the analogy of working with a person with a disability to that of solving a puzzle.

A person with a disability is a *person*, not a puzzle to be solved. People with disabilities are humans, with hopes, fears, and feelings just like anyone else. People with disabilities don't need to be solved; they need to be respected. They have a right to an education without degradation just like any other human. Make sure you do your best to treat them that way, and help ensure that those you meet treat them that way too.

Open and Accessible Materials

Traditional educational materials such as textbooks can be expensive. One way to decrease the cost of education while simultaneously increasing learner agency is for educators to choose materials that are available through an open license and are made in such a way that they are accessible to the widest range of individuals possible.

The Opportunities in Open Educational Resources

Open educational resources (OER) operate under the premise that educational resources should be available to the public for free, and that individuals using them should be allowed to use and redistribute them without limits. Switching to openly licensed educational materials has allowed school districts to use funding that would have otherwise gone to traditional, static textbooks for other needs, such as investing in technology. Open educational materials that are made in accessible formats in conjunction with technology can close equity gaps and empower individuals to take ownership of their learning.

Imagine a high school student with dyslexia who comes from a low-income family. He dreams of a life as a software engineer, perhaps working in the gaming industry. Unfortunately, the student learned early on that traditional school wasn't designed for him, as he struggled with the print-based materials all through his elementary and middle school years.

Currently, the path to his dream might look bleak or nigh impossible. He needs good grades and lots of money to get into college to earn a degree. He's already working after-school jobs, but that money goes toward the subsistence of his family and not into a college saving plan. In school, the materials presented to him in most classes are on paper. He does have a smartphone, but he's rarely allowed to use it, because most teachers deem it a distraction from the materials he struggles to read.

Socially, his friends are placing pressures on him that go against his desired path, but unable to see a light at the end of a different tunnel, he starts to make some less-than-positive choices.

Then, in his junior year, something changes. One of his educators only provides text-based materials that can be read aloud by a computer. The educator shows the entire class how to access the text via the technology in the school but encourages everyone to experiment with the functionality on their phones, to see if they can get their phones to read text aloud as well. Our student discovers that his phone has this functionality. The educator selects materials open for public consumption and shows the students where to find other such materials. Beyond digitally printed text, the educator shows the students how to access videos and podcasts—both available for free—to learn new content.

AWESOME INSIGHT

As the prevalence and availability of open education rises, what is one truly paying for when attending a college or university? One could argue that the value is the credit or diploma received rather than the knowledge and experience. Depending on the nature of the employment, additional certification from an established organization or government body might be necessary. Could it be feasible for someone to gain the skills necessary to achieve certification by using open education resources without attending (and paying for) a college degree?

Without relying on his reading ability, our student starts to listen to podcasts and text converted to audio. He listens as often as he can. He listens during study halls and on his way to work. He wishes every teacher provided content in this manner, because when he finds or is presented with materials this way, he enjoys learning. He starts to search out content of interest to him, including materials on software development, game design, and coding. Using more free tools on the internet, he begins to apply what he has learned during study hall to practice coding. College still seems unreachable, but at least he can now access content of interest.

One day, while listening to a podcast, he learns that one of the companies at which he dreams of working is hiring software engineers. Unbelievably, they are considering any applicant who can do the job, no matter how that individual acquired the skills. The human resources department at the company has realized that they have been limiting their talent pool by only considering people with college degrees. So they've widened their search criteria to include people who work hard and are good at problem solving but who haven't, for whatever reason, been able to attend college.

He doubles his efforts by using the free, open materials to practice, hone, and solidify his skills. Confident in his abilities based on the time he has spent learning both the necessary theory and practice, he applies for the job and gets an interview. He shares his story of gumption, grit, and perseverance during the conversational portion of the interview. He explains his disability and how he uses a combination of technology and open materials to find a way to circumnavigate traditional methodologies. He explains how he has found a way that works for him. He successfully completes the tasks set forth during the interview, impresses those doing the hiring, and lands his dream job. Proud of his work, he decides to focus on projects at the company that aid others. His access to accessible, open-source materials made his career a possibility.

#GoOpen

The US Department of Education has launched a campaign titled "#GoOpen," which encourages states, local educational agencies, and educators to switch to using openly licensed educational materials (tech.ed.gov/open). Innovative educational technology companies and nonprofit organizations are working with state and local educational leaders to share ideas and strategies, create new tools and resources, and provide professional-development opportunities that help educators locate, utilize, implement, create, and share open educational materials.

To support the #GoOpen initiative, the Obama administration partnered with the New York Public Library to develop an ebook reader application aptly named "Open eBooks" (openebooks.net). This application allows users to access thousands of free books on tablets or other mobile technologies, such as smartphones. The app is open to any educator, student, or administrator working or attending a Title I school, in a Department of Defense Education Activity school, any student with a disability, or any special educator.

Breaking the Cycle of Inaccessibility

Your school is looking to buy some stuff. Perhaps it is a new assessment tool; an on-demand math application with automatic leveling and cool video reinforcers that also integrate data collection for progress monitoring; or a some new copies of *Crime and Punishment* for the English department, because the current copies are looking pretty ratty. What does the process of purchasing those materials look like? What steps are involved?

First, the educators contact a vendor (or a vendor contacts the educators, planting the seed for the purchase in the first place). Next, the vendor might show off the product to the educators, demonstrating the various features while explaining—in detail—how their product will make education easier, better, faster, etc. The educator buys the new hotness, implements it in the class, and it works just as the vendor said it would ... for *most* of the students in the class.

Unfortunately, the new assessment tool wasn't designed to work with screen reading technology, and therefore, text-to-speech software won't work with it. The video animations in the math application don't come with captions, so the student with a hearing impairment can't listen to included audio. The new copies of *Crime and Punishment* are printed on dead trees, making it impossible for the students with dyslexia or visual impairments to adjust the font types, colors, and sizes, or easily convert it into an audio format.

Accommodations in the IEPs of these students dictate their need to have materials in a format that is accessible to them. To meet those requirements, the students with disabilities are pulled away from the other students so a staff member can read the text within that new assessment aloud. While all of the other students use the math application independently on mobile devices wherever they want, the student with the hearing impairment either misses out on the audio content or needs to spend time seeking out a staff member to ask for the creation of a transcription of the audio he is missing. A special educator needs to seek out a human-narrated or accessible digital version of *Crime and Punishment* for each student who requires it in a nonprint format. Precious time and resources are spent navigating inaccessible materials. Then, when it comes time to make the next purchase for more materials, the cycle starts all over again (see Figure 3.2).

The PALM Initiative

How do you stop this madness? How do you break the cycle of inaccessibility?

Imagine a world where the vendors themselves only sell accessible materials. Where whatever is being purchased is accessible to anyone and everyone. Where the materials, as part of the design, are developed with flexibility and variance of users in mind. And in this world, no educator needs to accommodate inaccessible materials. Every option made available for purchase is simply born accessible.

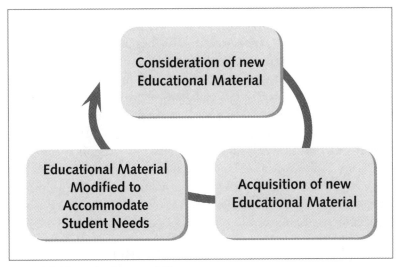

Figure 3.2 The cycle of inaccessibility.

Sure, that world sounds amazing, but so does riding a winged unicorn through a waterfall of chocolate sprinkles! Our reality is not a magical fantasy land where all our wishes come true. But could a world of accessibility become a reality? Could our choices, day by day, slowly change the landscape of existence? What steps could we take to create that world?

There is a strategy educators can use to inch toward that perfect world. It's called the Purchase Accessible Learning Materials (PALM) Initiative.

The Center for Applied Special Technology (CAST) is an organization on the forefront of Universal Design for Learning research and training. The organization also spearheads efforts to teach educators about the importance of implementing materials that are accessible to every learner. Recognizing this cycle of inaccessibility, CAST worked to develop a method for breaking it. The PALM Initiative invites educational institutions to ask questions of the vendor about accessibility before making a purchase and then only purchase materials that are born accessible (National Center on Accessible Educational Materials, 2013).

Imagine you are a vendor of the golden Thingamawhatchit. You've poured time and money into developing this bad boy, and you're ready to get school districts to purchase it. You even believe your Thingamawhatchit has the power to really solve some problems for teachers, and you're proud to have it take its place in the pantheon of educational tools. Your sales representative schedules a meeting to demonstrate the product to a team of educators at a local school and prepares a presentation to show off all the cool, whizbang features. The presentation is so good, you just *know* those educators won't be able to leave that meeting without ordering 20 Thingamawhatchits. Heck, they might even order the two-year subscription plan too! After all, it's just too good of a deal to pass up! You're convinced (or you've convinced yourself) that all the work, time, and money you've invested is going to come home to roost. The Thinga-mawhatchit had better sell because if it doesn't... Well, you don't want to think about the consequences of failure. Looking for a new job doesn't sound appealing.

As the vendor, you have a lot riding on the sale of the Thingamawhatchit, which means the educational institution holds the keys to the car. There is a lot of power to drive change forward when they dangle those keys in front of you. When the meeting and presentation by the sales representative takes place, the educators are impressed, but they ask some serious questions about the accessibility of the Thingamawhatchit, including the following:

- Can the text be read aloud?

- Can that text be enlarged?

- Can the background change colors?

- Can the entire contrast be shifted using various background and text colors?

- When audio plays, is there a corresponding text representation of that sound?

- If the audio is an alarm, is there a visual or physical prompt that can be set to display simultaneously, like a strobing light or a vibration?

- When images are presented, do they have corresponding text describing the picture?

- Can this text also be presented in audio format?

- When video plays, is there a corresponding optional audio track that can be played, describing the action in the video?

- Is directly selecting items on the Thingamawhatchit the only way to interact with it or does the user interface have multiple input options, such as using a switch?

- Is the Thingamawhatchit portable? If so, is it light enough to be carried by most children? If not, can it be attached to a mount that can be placed on a wheelchair?

If you switch your role to that of an educator, it is your job to advocate for every student, in the present and in the future. This means the Thingamawhatchit must meet the needs of every situation. Understand the scope of the potential purchase: If someone fails to ask questions about the functionality of the Thingamawhatchit, a catastrophic chain of events will occur, costing your district time, money, and energy. Fortunately, this can be avoided by simply asking questions about accessibility before the purchase is made.

There is a giant, not-so-invisible bag of cash sitting on the table in front of these two parties. The vendor desperately needs it, which gives the teacher tremendous leverage. Refusal to make the purchase without affirmative answers to questions about accessibility causes the vendor to return to his company with feedback for the developers, entering into discussions about how to modify the Thingamawhatchit to make it more accessible to all potential users. Further, when the company begins to develop its next product, it has learned how and why to build the product with accessibility in mind from the onset, rather than making a retrofit.

When educators repeatedly demand accessible products and uphold that vote with the educational agency's wallet, they can help break the cycle of inaccessibility. By asking a few important questions and then only spending funds on products that were born accessible, educators can send an ongoing message that has the power to push the entire market toward one of inclusivity.

The CALM Initiative

The PALM Initiative references purchasing educational materials. Educators might have the impression that they don't have a say in what gets purchased—that an administrator might make a choice to purchase materials, which then trickles down to the individual educational experience designers.

However, educational experience designers are continuously making decisions about instructional materials. Sometimes, these decisions are related to or have influence over a purchase, but more commonly, the decision is not directly related to a dollar amount. Instead, it is choosing which materials should be made available to the students in a given educational environment. Educational experience designers take the iniative to adopt a philosophy whereby they only choose to use materials that are accessible to the widest range of student abilities. This principle is known as the Choose Accessible Learning Materials (CALM) Initiative and is broader in scope than the PALM Initiative, as educational experience designers apply it to *every* choice they make with regard to materials. And when an educational experience designer only chooses accessible materials, it sends the message that every experience is meant to be for every student.

AWESOME INSIGHT

Start a campaign in your district to spread the PALM and CALM Initiatives. Invite educators to sign a pledge decreeing that they will only choose and purchase materials born accessible. Inspire and educate administrators to be the ones who ask these driving questions. Work to have a seat at the table when purchasing decisions are being made. If nothing else, a pledge increases the awareness of the problem and the search for a potential solution.

Before selecting any instructional material, an educational experience designer considers the needs of those students with disabilities from the outset as an integral aspect of the design. Questions about accessibility of the material are at the forefront of the design and not an afterthought for a different educator to modify. A goal for an educational experience designer is to construct an environment in which he or she can say, "In this classroom, every resource, material, or tool I use will be selected based on what is accessible to all of my students." This exemplifies to every stakeholder that accessibility and inclusivity is part of the fabric woven into every lesson. Making an individual commitment (and sticking to it) moves the needle of progress and sustainable change. It also sets an example that others can follow (see Figure 3.3).

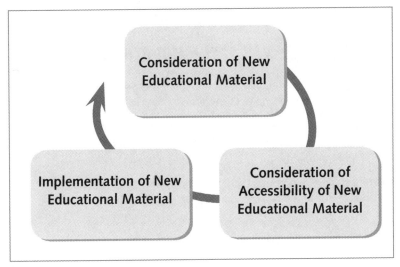

Figure 3.3 The cycle of accessibility.

Using What Everyone Else Uses

While some services are meant to be accessed exclusively by students with disabilities, the need to offer separate services can be mitigated when an educational experience designer uses materials that are born accessible for everyone. Beyond the inclusionary benefits, choosing accessible products has additional practical, positive aspects. Choosing accessibility decreases costs in service fees and staff time spent in learning, navigating, and maintaining the services. Choosing accessibility means not wrestling with an entirely separate set of tools used exclusively for students with disabilities. On the contrary, the educational experience designer has selected a varied set of materials from sources that provide accessible solutions for everyone.

It is important to note that despite a concerted effort to choose materials that are born accessible and the provision of a variety of options based on student preference, specialized services and technologies designed for people with highly specific needs will continue to be necessary to help people with disabilities interact with objects and people in their environment. Still, educational experience designers should attempt to select materials that work for everyone before considering the implementation of something specialized.

"I DON'T GIVE STUDENTS ACCOMMODATIONS"

Mrs. Sheehan was confused. She honestly wasn't understanding what the older gentleman standing before her was talking about.

"This student has a visual impairment, Mrs. Sheehan. She has low vision, but she can see if the items are large enough. What part of that do you not understand? She has trouble seeing the board."

Did this man in his suit and tie honestly think she didn't know that? She'd had this student in her class for two months and knew her well. So, what was this guy getting at?

"I know she does," was all she could muster, confusion clinging to each word.

"If you present things on the board and she has a visual impairment, then how does she see it? You have to provide her with an accommodation so she can have access to the material like everyone else."

Mrs. Sheehan still wasn't getting it. Why would having low vision mean this student should have some sort of accommodation? Whoever this man was, he wasn't going to change her mind about that. She had her rules and this one was unbreakable.

"I'm sorry, but in my room, I don't do accommodations. My room is an accommodation-free zone. That's just how it is. That's how it has always been, and that's how it's going to remain."

"You do realize federal law dictates that you provide her with the necessary accommodations, don't you?" the man snorted, eyebrows furrowing. "You can't just deny her access to her education because your classroom rule prohibits it!"

And then, all at once, it clicked with Mrs. Sheehan. She finally understood the point the man was driving at. The pieces fell into place. She had met people like this man before. He was old school.

"Sir, thank you for your feedback—I get what you're saying. Every student has a right to a free appropriate public education, and this student has an IEP outlining what she needs. Is that accurate?"

"Yes!" the man sighed in relief. "Exactly."

A smile spread on Mrs. Sheehan's face.

"Here's what you don't understand," she explained. "The information presented on the board is also online. When I do review content from a slidedeck or multimedia slideshow, this student, or any other student, can choose to use their own device or one of the school's provisioned devices to access the content in real time. She can zoom in, annotate, or even go back later and review the video recording I make of each lesson. All the content is fully accessible online, with multiple options for how to access it.

"Sir, the reason she doesn't need an accommodation is simple: in my room, the instruction is designed so that everyone has access to what they need in the format in which they need it, disability or not."

PART II

HOW TO CONSIDER ASSISTIVE TECHNOLOGY FOR EVERYBODY

CHAPTER 4

Assistive Technology (Re)Defined

How does technology—specifically, assistive technology—fit into contemporary educational practice? Assistive technology is a concept defined by federal law in the United States, and its consideration is a necessary component at every IEP meeting. As the very nature of public education undergoes change as outlined in the previous chapters of this book, so, too, must practices in assistive technology. Before we can discuss what those changes might be, a common definition needs to be established.

In this chapter, you'll:

1. Examine the definition of assistive technology and the implications of its interpretation.

2. Explore who is qualified to provide assistive technology devices and services.

ISTE STANDARDS ADDRESSED

ISTE Standards for Educators 2c. Model for colleagues the identification, exploration, evaluation, curation, and adoption of new digital resources and tools for learning.

ISTE Standards for Educators 5a. Use technology to create, adapt, and personalize learning experiences that foster independent learning and accommodate learner differences and needs.

ISTE Standards for Educators 6b. Manage the use of technology and student learning strategies in digital platforms, virtual environments, hands-on makerspaces, and/or in the field.

ISTE Standards for Educators 7a. Provide alternative ways for students to demonstrate competency and reflect on their learning by using technology.

What the Heck Is Assistive Technology Anyway?

In the United States, federal law Public Law (PL) 108-446, the Individuals with Disabilities Education Improvement Act of 2004, defines the term *assistive technology* in relation to public schools. The term is broken down into two integral parts: the first is "assistive technology device" and the second is "assistive technology service."

According to this law, "assistive technology device" means "any item, piece of equipment, or product system, whether acquired commercially off the shelf, modified, or customized, that is used to increase, maintain, or improve functional capabilities of a child with a disability." It excludes devices that are surgically implanted.

Also, according to this law, "assistive technology service" is defined as "any service that directly assists a child with a disability in the selection, acquisition, or use of an assistive technology device." The term includes:

a. "the evaluation of the needs of such child, including a functional evaluation of the child in the child's customary environment;

b. "purchasing, leasing, or otherwise providing for the acquisition of assistive technology devices by such child;

c. "selecting, designing, fitting, customizing, adapting, applying, maintaining, repairing, or replacing assistive technology devices;

d. "coordinating and using other therapies, interventions, or services with assistive technology devices, such as those associated with existing education and rehabilitation plans and programs;

e. "training or technical assistance for such child, or, where appropriate, the family of such child; and

f. "training or technical assistance for professionals (including individuals providing education and rehabilitation services), employers, or other individuals who provide services to, employ, or are otherwise substantially involved in the major life functions of such child."

When establishing your policies, procedures, and practices, refer to this law for support.

An Individualized Education Program (IEP) team is charged with the task of defining what a student needs to guarantee a free appropriate public education including assistive technology (devices and services). The IEP team decides, outlines, and documents what the student requires. If a piece of technology is one of the student's requirements, then the IEP team should document this need in the IEP.

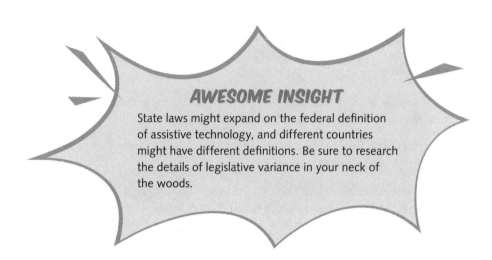

AWESOME INSIGHT

State laws might expand on the federal definition of assistive technology, and different countries might have different definitions. Be sure to research the details of legislative variance in your neck of the woods.

The Assistive Technology Act of 1998

The Technology-Related Assistance for Individuals with Disabilities Act was first passed in 1988 (PL 100-407). It was reauthorized in 1994 (PL 103-218) and again in 1998 (PL 105-394), when it was retitled the Assistive Technology Act. The purpose of the law was to increase the access to and availability of technology used by people with disabilities. The act allowed for the provision of federal funds to states to create technology assistance programs. Every state and territory of the United States created and continues to maintain statewide programs, which have the potential to provide valuable support to educational agencies and school districts. The people employed through the Assistive Technology Act can also be valuable allies in the effort to build capacity within an institution.

Beyond the Assistive Technology Act of 1998, there has been other legislation that calls attention to accessibility. This includes Section 504 of the Rehabilitation Act of 1973 (PL 93-112), the Americans with Disabilities Act of 1990 (PL 101-336), Section 508 of the Rehabilitation Act Amendments of 1998 (29 USC 794d), the Individuals with Disabilities Education Act (PL 101-476), the No Child Left Behind Act of 2001 (PL 107-110), and the Assistive Technology Act of 2004 (PL 108-364).

These laws help establish and maintain the necessity of access to technology for students with disabilities. Awareness of these laws draws attention to the notion that consideration of technology for students with disabilities is a fundamental necessity in contemporary education.

Any Item and Any Service

A common element in both parts of the definition of assistive technology is the very first word, *any:* "any item" or "any service." This small, three-letter word encompasses a universe of options because it literally means "without limitations." Imagination is the only boundary when it comes to brainstorming potential solutions. And anyone who helps a student select, obtain, and then use that item is providing an assistive technology service.

Every Discussion About a Tool

If an assistive technology service is defined as "any service that directly assists a child with a disability in the selection, acquisition, or use of an assistive technology device" and an assistive technology device is "any item ... that is used to increase, maintain, or improve functional capabilities of a child with a disability," then *any* discussion pertaining to the implementation of *any* feature or *any* function of *any* tool used by *any* student with *any* disability is an assistive technology service.

The Definition of "Assistive Technology Device"

The federal definition of an assistive technology device causes a conundrum: What is the difference between educational/instructional technology and assistive technology? What makes something shift from everyday technology to assistive technology? Isn't all technology, by definition, designed to be assistive?

The Confusing Use of "Used"

The verb *used* is a point of confusion surrounding the federal definition of an assistive technology device ("any item ... that is *used* to increase, maintain, or improve functional capabilities of a child with a disability"). Consider the word *used* in relation to the following example juxtaposing two fictional students: one with a disability and one without. The federal definition does not make any presumptions about the type of tool used or the task the tool is helping the user achieve. For this example, let's consider text-to-speech as the function of the tool.

Student one: a student with a disability *used* the text-to-speech function of a device to listen to text being read aloud. Here, we call the device and its text-to-speech functionality "assistive technology" because the person using it has been identified as a student with a disability.

Student two: a student without a disability *used* the text-to-speech function of a device to listen to text being read aloud. Although the device is assisting this student, because this student does not have an identified disability, the device is not considered assistive technology. We call the device and its text-to-speech functionality "technology."

The only difference between these two students, who both *used* the exact same device in the same way and for identical purposes, is that the student with the disability might require the device to complete the task and the student without the disability might not. *Need* may be the only difference. When an IEP team meets to discuss what is necessary to ensure a free appropriate public education, they are determining what a student *requires*. The question of what a person uses versus what a person requires can cause confusion about what is and what is not considered assistive technology. Regardless of what it is called, the responsibility of the IEP team—to determine and document what is necessary—is unchanged.

The Definition of "Assistive Technology Device" Re-envisioned

What can we do to fix the potential problem with the definition of an assistive technology device? Although there may be more solutions, here are two options that might solve the conundrum.

A Practical Option

The first option might be to simply advocate for a wording change in the federal definition by swapping the word *used* for *needs*, or *requires*. The definition of "assistive technology device" could read "any item, piece of equipment, or product system, whether acquired commercially off the shelf, modified, or customized, that *is required* to increase, maintain, or improve the functional capabilities of children with disabilities." Using this definition, any item used by a student, whether they have a disability or not, would just be considered technology. This would represent a more accurate distinction between what makes a piece of equipment technology versus what makes it assistive technology.

A Visionary Option

Could we envision a world where every student has access to whatever he or she needs to achieve his or her individual educational goals regardless of ability or disability? Could we envision a possible future where disability itself isn't something considered separately?

Imagine a future so inclusive that laws governing disability aren't needed, because the very notion of disability doesn't exist. Everyone living in this society might see people as bodies of potential energy capable of achieving anything if only given access to the appropriate tools. Could we imagine a society so inclusive that the adjective *assistive* is no longer required as a distinction and is therefore abandoned? In this culture, everything and anything a person uses in the process of learning, whether that person has a disability or not, would just be called "technology." Technology used by anyone empowers every individual to achieve his or her potential and beyond (see Figure 4.1).

Figure 4.1 The endless struggle between accepting where we are and reaching for where we want to be (created using http://pixton.com).

Noun, Not Adjective

One step toward building a more inclusive world is related to how we choose the words to describe that world. The term *assistive technology* is used in front of the words *device* and *service*. In both cases, it acts as a qualifier, or an adjective, describing the word that follows it. What type of device is it? It is an *assistive technology* device. What type of service is it? It is an *assistive technology* service. However, "assistive technology," when not used to modify a noun, is a compound noun itself. In fact, the *idea* of the entire definition is meant to describe assistive technology's usage as a noun. "Assistive technology *device*" and "assistive technology *service*" are both used to describe the definition of assistive technology. What is assistive technology? It is both a device and a service. Since both "device" and "service" act to qualify the overarching definition of assistive technology, *assistive technology* should only be used as a noun.

What benefit does it serve to add the qualifier *assistive technology* as an adjective to describe nouns such as *support, tool, initiative, product,* or *team*? Using the qualifier of *assistive technology* before these nouns implies that there is a difference between that item with and without the qualifier. For example, saying "we provide assistive technology supports" implies that there are supports that are not assistive technology. It may be true that there are two types of supports—assistive technology supports and non-assistive technology supports—but what purpose does that serve? Does using the term as an adjective to describe the function clarify that it is exclusively for people with disabilities? If a goal of special education is to create a more inclusive society where people with disabilities aren't viewed separately, does the use of the term *assistive technology* to qualify nouns help or hinder the cause?

What unintended message is sent when you call something a "support" versus an "assistive technology support"? What benefit is there to calling something an "assistive technology tool" as opposed to just calling it a "tool"? What connotation is implied when you call the initiative you are building an "assistive technology initiative"? Consider carefully how to use the term and, whenever possible, use it only as a noun.

Funding Foundation

Although it might be idealistic to abolish the term *assistive* from our collective lexicon as an adjective before *technology*, it is highly impractical and improbable for this to occur anytime soon. Current funding schemes work in such a way to provide financial restitution for minority groups, including people with disabilities. Funding based on the distinction and qualification of a person having a disability attempts to ensure equal access for people with disabilities, marching society onward toward inclusive practices for all.

Is Assistive Technology a Field of Practice?

Universal Design for Learning (UDL) is an idea or framework with principles that can be at the center of every instructional lesson. It is woven into the very fabric of what it means to be an inclusive educator. As each educator continues on his or her own professional journey, each might become more skilled in implementing the principles of UDL, but it is not its own field of practice.

Positions might exist in which educators trained in the ways of UDL might serve as coaches to other educators who want to or need to learn more, but this doesn't need to be someone who holds a certification in UDL. Instead, it can be any educator who has demonstrated the ability to design and deliver universally designed educational experiences. Although individual certifications for UDL are being considered by a diverse group of organizations convened by CAST and the UDL Implementation and Research group, this certification is not necessary to implement UDL principles; it is intended to be a credential an educator can add to his or her résumé. More importantly, they are considering offering institution-level credentialing so individual schools and entire school districts can be accredited as schools that embrace and utilize the principles of universal design in their everyday practice.

Like UDL, selecting, acquiring, and implementing technology to support a student doesn't need to be a separate field of practice. If this were true, then assistive technology itself should not be considered a separate field of practice. Helping to make decisions regarding technology is just part of what it means to be a contemporary educational experience designer. Individuals simply have varying degrees of experience working with different technologies.

Exterminator Experience

If you wage war on some ants that have invaded your kitchen and succeed in expunging them from your home, does that make you an exterminator? Most would probably argue that pest removal is a profession, and just because you killed a few ants doesn't make you some sort of expert in killing ants. However, what if a few months later, you find an infestation of mice that you relocate? Then, a week after that, you help your neighbor spray some chemicals around the outside of his house to keep spiders out? A bit later, as tales of your exploits spread, friends and acquaintances start writing you with questions about how to get rid of their own critters. Before long, you're doing research and learning more details about creepy-crawly control than you ever thought you would!

You, on purpose or accidentally, have learned a new skill. In fact, you've become such an expert that when your least-favorite neighbor (the one who lets her dog bark into the wee hours of the night) tells you about how she hired a licensed exterminator who overcharged for his services, you tell her that you would have helped in exchange for one night of her bringing her dog in. Further, when she shows you the bill and it states the chemical used to get rid of the termites, you instantly recognize that you would have chosen a less toxic yet equally effective pesticide.

At what point along the path of learning does one move from novice to amateur to expert in any given field? What distinguishes you, a person with lots of experience in extermination, from a professional whose job is extermination? Is it the exchange of money for services? Is it the fact that one person likely requires certification or a license from some public or private entity? If a person paid to take the examination to obtain certification and then paid even more money to obtain a license, does that mean this person is now knowledgeable in all things related to extermination?

Could someone who has not pursued certification and licensure still know as much or something different about extermination? With so much knowledge and research available to the public, are licensure and certification the only things that differentiate someone with formal training and those with an "I can learn how to do it myself" attitude? Do these questions extend to other professions as well, such as plumbing, car repair, or styling hair (see Figure 4.2)?

Figure 4.2 Who is qualified to use a fire extinguisher? (Created using toondoo.com.)

If You Give a Speech Therapist a Communication Device...

Consider this example of technology and expertise acquisition:

If you give a speech therapist a communication device (along with some advice on how to use it), she'll want to start using the device with a student with a language impairment. And because she knows about language development, she'll want to show the occupational therapist too.

The occupational therapist will ask about placement. When you talk about placement of the device, she might suggest a keyguard if the student needs one—the keyguard will help the student target and press the buttons. The student might start using language to communicate if people model on the device too, and he'll want everyone to model language to him.

When the student starts using the device, he'll want to use it everywhere. He'll want to use it when he is in his stander; and when he's in his stander, his physical therapist might see him using it. She'll want to use it with him too, but she'll probably need some help learning how.

When the physical therapist asks for help, the speech therapist will give her some advice; and she'll probably meet with her in person. When the training is over, the physical therapist will probably want the speech therapist to do a workshop for all the other physical therapists. The speech therapist will likely say yes and plan a training, and you'll probably want to attend.

When you go to the training, you'll bring your video camera. You'll record the session and put it online. When the speech therapist sees the video, she'll like it and want you to record more trainings. Then she'll share all the videos on social media. When people watch them, they'll share them too!

Some of the people who see the videos will be other educators, and they'll know other students with language impairments. If they are working directly with these students, they'll want a communication device to go with them.

In this example, consider the following:

- Who suggested the keyguard?

- How did the student get the stander?

- Who gave the speech therapist the device to be put in place? What was this person's role?

- Could the speech therapist have been the one to get the device in the first place? If not for this student, what about the next?

- The speech therapist certainly seemed qualified. What if the student needed another piece of equipment not mentioned in the story?

The communication device, the keyguard, and the stander are all assistive technologies, yet in most cases, the people making suggestions and then determinations for the implementation of a device do not have "assistive technology" in their job title. Instead, they hold certifications in their own respective fields of practice, and they infuse technology based on those credentials. One does not need to have the words "assistive technology" in her or his job title to suggest or implement assistive technology.

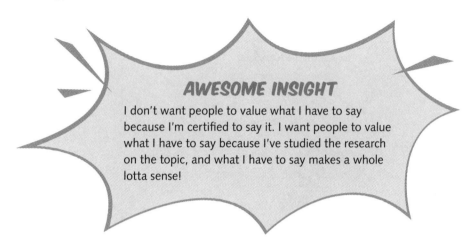

AWESOME INSIGHT

I don't want people to value what I have to say because I'm certified to say it. I want people to value what I have to say because I've studied the research on the topic, and what I have to say makes a whole lotta sense!

Anyone and Everyone

Knowledge of and experience with technology, assistive or otherwise, is a spectrum. Everyone has some knowledge about technology that could be used to help students learn, including the students themselves! Professionals grow their knowledge base with each situation they work through.

A person's knowledge and skill level about different functions or aspects of technology can be charted on a spider or radar chart. This type of chart is a graphical method of displaying quantitative variables. Professionals (and students) can chart how comfortable they are with any number of different technologies, illustrating their strengths and where they need to learn more.

For example, a professional might have years of experience supporting students who are using an augmentative/alternative communication (AAC) device to learn language but have very little experience working with tools related to literacy and reading. Another professional might have loads of experience with literacy and reading supports but have virtually no experience with augmentative/alternative communication devices. *Both*, however, have experience using technology to help students with disabilities. *Both* know assistive technology. The only difference is in what they know.

Anyone and everyone (parents, students, and educators) can rank their abilities on a spider or radar chart because anyone and everyone has some knowledge about what might help a student achieve their educational goals (see Figures 4.3 through 4.6).

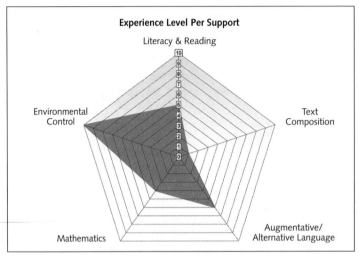

Figure 4.3 An individual with the most experience in working with environmental-control supports.

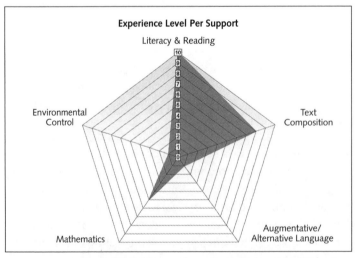

Figure 4.4 An individual with the most experience working with literacy and reading supports.

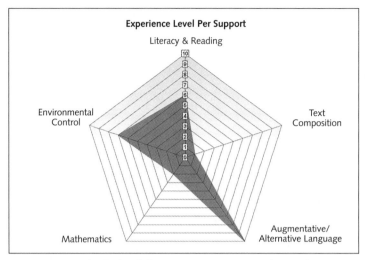

Figure 4.5 An individual with the most experience in working with augmentative/alternative language supports.

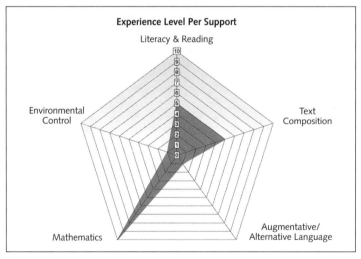

Figure 4.6 An individual with the most experiences in working with mathematical supports.

CHAPTER **5**

Principles Guiding Consideration of (Assistive) Technology

Educational experience designers are constantly considering the access needs of every student during the design, implementation, and reflection phases of every educational experience. They think about how technology can be used and provided to present every student with access based on his or her individual needs and preferences. Then, while the students are engaged in an educational experience, the educational experience designer might recognize that a single student or group of students might need access to something different, new, or novel. With flexibility built into the design of the experience, the educational experience designer can shift gears and provide access to additional or supplemental options, including the technology needed.

Even if every educational experience is designed with every participant in mind, federal law dictates that the technological needs of students with disabilities needs to be considered and documented. According to the Individuals with Disabilities Education Improvement Act (PL 108-446), every Individualized Education Program team is required "to consider whether the child needs assistive technology devices and services." Consideration means giving careful thought to what a student needs in order to access her or his education. Educational experience designers, IEP teams, and those who support both can use the information in this chapter to guide this process.

In this chapter, you'll:

1. Learn a consistent process for considering, selecting, and documenting the technology needs of every student.

2. Practice how to choose technology based on what restricts the student the least.

ISTE STANDARDS ADDRESSED

ISTE Standards for Educators 2a. Shape, advance, and accelerate a shared vision for empowered learning with technology by engaging with education stakeholders.

ISTE Standards for Educators 2b. Advocate for equitable access to educational technology, digital content, and learning opportunities to meet the diverse needs of all students.

ISTE Standards for Educators 2c. Model for colleagues the identification, exploration, evaluation, curation, and adoption of new digital resources and tools for learning.

ISTE Standards for Educators 4a. Dedicate planning time to collaborate with colleagues to create authentic learning experiences that leverage technology.

How to Determine and Document Technology Needs

IEP teams typically have all the skills, experience, and expertise to make informed decisions without assistance from a third party. When an IEP team meets to discuss which tools and strategies need to be put in place to ensure a free appropriate public education, they are using student performance evidence to arrive at different decisions regarding each student's education. Members of the IEP team work through the process of generating accommodations and assign people responsibility for the acquisition and implementation of whatever is determined to be necessary.

To do this, the IEP team members can use a structured model to decide what a student needs by examining the student, environment, and tasks, making the necessary adjustments to the environment, tasks, and tools when appropriate.

Ensuring Access to a Free Appropriate Public Education

In the United States, students with disabilities are guaranteed "a free appropriate public education" (or FAPE) as outlined in the Individuals with Disabilities Education Improvement Act of 2004 (PL 108-446). A free appropriate public education is defined as "special education and related services that:

a. "have been provided at public expense, under public supervision and direction, and without charge;

b. "meet the standards of the state educational agency;

c. "include an appropriate preschool, elementary school, or secondary school education in the state involved; and

d. "are provided in conformity with the Individualized Education Program required under section 614(d)."

It is the responsibility of the IEP team to determine what is necessary to ensure a free appropriate public education. Discussing what a student needs includes the consideration of technology.

The Individuals with Disabilities Education Improvement Act also indicates that special-education services, including assistive technology, are to be provided at no cost to the family. When an IEP is finalized, whatever is required for the student to receive a free appropriate public education, including the student's assistive technology needs, means what it literally says—that it's "free" to the parents. This does not, however, preclude parents from purchasing technology and providing it for their child to use in the educational environment if they so choose.

Determining Needs with the SETT Framework

Educator Joy Zabala (joyzabala.com) has created the SETT Framework to help IEP teams consider the needs of a student with a disability. SETT is an acronym for Student, Environments, Tasks, and Tools. The SETT Framework can be used to guide an IEP team through the process of determining what changes might be necessary to ensure a free appropriate public education. To illustrate how an IEP team can use the framework, consider the following example.

Creating A Shared Perspective

An IEP team meets to discuss what is required to support a high school student with a specific learning disability who is demonstrating difficulty with learning mathematics. Every team member comes with an individual perspective about the student's abilities and performance, the learning environments, and the tasks the student is expected or hopes to do. Often, individuals come with ideas about the tools—devices and other supports—that are needed. The SETT Framework is used to help the individual perspectives shift to one that is shared before trying to determine which tools will help the student do what she needs to do when and where she needs to do it. At the start of the IEP meeting, a chart of the SETT Framework is displayed. It includes a quadrant to outline data points regarding the student, the environments, the tasks, and the tools. Throughout the meeting, the team adds information to each section of the chart as each relevant piece of information is discussed.

Making the Shared Perspective Explicit

During the review of the PLAAFP (Present Levels of Academic Achievement and Functional Performance, or "present levels") portion of the meeting, in which the team discusses the student's strengths and areas of concern, it is revealed that the student continues to have trouble completing mathematical problems consistently. This has been a known area of concern, and goals related to math content have been included in prior IEPs. The IEP team notes this along with other information pertinent to the student, such as revelations from standardized assessments, notations from her current educators. These and other insights from the student herself, such as her preference to receive instruction presented on the interactive whiteboard, to complete work in small groups, or to follow video models to help solve a problem, are noted in the "student" field of the SETT Framework chart.

After the IEP team has discussed and outlined the goals, the meeting turns to the discussion of services. As part of this discussion, the IEP team discusses the least restrictive environment (the LRE, per the IDEA). Information about the student's environment, such as tools already available to her, are noted in the "environments" section of the SETT chart. These items include how she chooses to be close to the interactive whiteboard; the arrangement of desks, which is in rows; her access to a graphing scientific calculator; and her ownership of a personal mobile device.

It is also noted how, for her entire academic career, the task of completing mathematical notations has been conducted in a handwritten format. This item is listed in the "tasks" section of the chart.

Analyzing the Chart

When the IEP team turns its discussion to the accommodations necessary for the student to meet the goals, the team reviews what has been listed in the student, environments, and tasks portions of the chart. Based on the items in these lists, the IEP team constructs a fourth list of potential tools. It is suggested that the student access mobile applications that allow her to scan math problems to check her answers. The team agrees that the student should feel welcomed to use her own personal device to use these applications but also have access to a device made available by the school district.

The IEP team also suggests that the student explore the completion of mathematical notation digitally. Digital notation tools that would allow the student to construct problems by typing them are recommended, just to rule out any factors that might be caused by legibility. The task of completing the math problems would be the same as in the past, but the modality the student is using to complete the assignment would be different.

Documenting Determinations

Accommodations are crafted based on the analysis of the chart. In the case of this student, an accommodation related to ensuring she has access to a device with the ability to scan math problems is documented with the purpose of allowing her to check her work. Another accommodation referencing her access to a digital notation tool is written.

The educator designing the mathematical instructional experiences takes note of the IEP and considers alterations to the tasks as well. He attempts to design lessons in a way that the student experiences how the math is practically applied to solve authentic problems, and he finds that the accommodations that have been provided for the student with a disability are useful to many other students as well.

A Store for Everything: Pros and Cons of Consideration Guides

Imagine a magical store that has everything. A shopper can arrive and literally buy anything in his or her imagination. You want a flying purple polka-dotted teddy bear with two horns and sunglasses? Got it. Need salt-and-pepper shakers shaped like unicorns wearing headphones and playing reggae music? It's here. Looking for an automated, self-guided, camera-equipped lawnmower that also shovels snow, rakes leaves, and power-washes the house? Just check the outdoor power equipment section.

Actual stores—both brick-and-mortar and online—are limiting. Even vast online retail databases can't have everything and anything one might need.

According to the federal definition of an assistive technology device, any item could be considered. To help IEP teams compare options, different institutions have generated lists or databases with ideas of tools and strategies. These lists are commonly known as "assistive technology consideration guides" and can be employed in various academic areas. Some local education agencies have links to these guides built right into their IEP system for the team's use. But like a retail store's inventory, there are limits as to what can fit in these guides.

Limits, however, can be a good thing. One can get lost in the Sea of Indecision without some guidelines, waypoints, or a map. No consideration guide can encompass every possible tool and strategy—but they aren't meant to. The purpose of the guide is to provide talking points and ideas, not to catalog every single option in existence.

Whether or not the IEP team uses a consideration guide, the approach for tool selection entails various degrees of the same process. The IEP team develops goals to ensure a free appropriate public education and generates a list of items and actions that might be required to meet those goals. Then the IEP team decides which items and actions are required, and documents them on the IEP.

Building Capacity Through the Consideration Process

The primary goal of any technology consideration process is to come to a conclusion about the needs of the student. However, the process has a secondary objective as well: to choose the most cost-effective approach to refining the process. Costs associated with developing and maintaining this process might be measured both financially and in time.

The process can also work to empower educators to become increasingly more confident in their own abilities to research, select, acquire, and provide what a student needs. The more opportunities individuals have at determining what a student needs, the better they become at the entire process.

Those assisting in the process have an opportunity to facilitate and expedite the learning of individuals working directly with the student. Coaching IEP team members through the process is an opportunity to build skills and knowledge exponentially—so that these skills are carried over and applied to the next situation and the next, and so on. This is how capacity is built.

Depending on how services are structured in your neck of the woods, the model for determining needs might vary slightly from the one outlined in this book. The model outlined here is meant to bring about a level of confidence within the IEP team members, with the ultimate goal of removing their need to ask for assistance. It is meant to empower them to make their own decisions. (Keep in mind that it may be necessary to adjust this model based on the different needs of your institution.)

No matter the variations in the process and model, certain principles should remain constant and consistent throughout. One commonality that appears often is the use of the concepts included in the SETT Framework, although the labeling may be different. If unfamiliar with this framework, it might be beneficial for members of the IEP team to use the framework explicitly and methodically, providing details in each of the four areas. Systematically documenting relevant aspects of the student, environments, and tasks can help participants arrive upon decisions pertaining to the necessary tools for and alterations to the environments and tasks. Another commonality amongst every model variation: when deciding which changes to put in place, be sure the change is the one that would be the least restrictive to the student.

First Function, Then Tool, Then Documentation

Tools come and go, and your favorite tool might already be facing imminent doom. The smaller and more independent the company that produces the tool, the more likely it is that it might not be long for this world. Alternatively, the tool might be so good that one of the big companies will snatch it up and buy it out. When a company is purchased, the tool might be saved, shelved, or integrated into an existing tool. The technology industry can be fickle, uncertain, and unreliable—unfortunately.

What persists beyond the tool is the function. Why did a student use (need) that tool in the first place? When the IEP team determines a need, what purpose does that need serve? The purpose or function of a tool is what really matters, and it is likely that there are other tools out there that provide the same or similar functions.

For example, word processing is a function. The purpose of a word processor is to help users produce written text. Microsoft Word and Google Docs are examples of tools that provide this function. Likewise, text-to-speech is a function. The purpose of a text-to-speech tool is to help someone consume or comprehend text material. Read&Write for Google Chrome and Snap&Read Universal (for Google Chrome and iPad) are two examples of text-to-speech tools. In contemporary education, there are numerous functions that prove useful for students in general.

Individual Feature Matching

Using the SETT Framework helps an IEP identify which functions might be necessary for a student, but it only takes you so far. In some cases, the SETT Framework leads you to a necessary function, but the IEP team might not be sure about which specific tool should be implemented to provide that function. When this is unclear, a commonly used practice is to generate a list of specific needs and then a corresponding list of potential technologies that might meet those needs.

Imagine a table with multiple columns. The first column might contain a list of student needs, and the top row might list names or types of devices. Any item being considered could be listed in this top row, with each device being the heading for a new column. Checkmarks (or other indicators) could be placed in the device column next to each need if the tool meets that need.

Following this process, a team can systematically evaluate and consider different options to provide the items that meet the greatest number (if not all) of the needs.

This technique of intervention selection is known as "feature matching": the needs of the student are matched to the features of the options being considered to determine which technologies meet the most needs. This long-standing, legacy practice has helped many students get the devices necessary to ensure a free appropriate public education (see Tables 5.1 and 5.2).

Table 5.1 Blank Feature-Matching Chart

Needs	Option 1	Option 2	Option 3
Need 1			
Need 2			
Need 3			
Need 4			

Table 5.2 Sample Feature-Matching Chart

Needs	Option 1	Option 2	Option 3
Text-to-Speech with Highlighting	X		X
Word Prediction	X		X
Voice Recording	X		X
Graphic Organizer		X	X

Document What Is Necessary

Once an IEP team has decided what is necessary, it needs to document these requirements in the IEP. *The Practical (and Fun) Guide to Assistive Technology in Public Schools* (Bugaj & Norton-Darr, 2014) details how the consideration of assistive technology overlaps with the consideration of accommodations and how to document them as accommodations within an Individualized Education Program when considering this assistive technology. Basically, whenever an IEP team is discussing which items a student needs to guarantee a free appropriate public education and which actions might be necessary to implement these items, it is considering assistive technology. And whatever item the IEP team decides is necessary should be documented.

If Needed, Write It In (Whether It Is Universally Available or Not)

The availability of a tool does not negate the need for it to be written in as an accommodation. If a student needs it, whether it is something already in the environment or something that needs to be acquired, note it on the IEP document. This way, anyone unfamiliar to the learning environment can read the documentation and know what the IEP team has determined to be a need. This documentation is particularly helpful when a student transitions from setting to setting and when sharing the documentation with third parties, such as physicians or private therapists.

HOW A FUNCTION BECOMES AN ACCOMMODATION (A SCHOOLHOUSE ROCK! PARODY)

Boy: Whew! You sure gotta climb a lot of steps to get to this IEP meeting here in school. But I wonder who that sad little scrap of paper is?

Function (singing):
I'm just a function.
Yes, I'm only a function,
and I'm sitting here on the IEP table.
Well, it's a long, long journey
to the IEP table.
It's a long, long wait
while I'm sitting in committee.
But I know I'll be an accommodation someday—
at least, I hope and pray that I will.
But today, I am still just a function.

Boy: Gee, Function, you certainly have a lot of patience and courage.

Function: Well, I got this far. When I started, I wasn't even a function; I was just an idea to solve some sort of problem. Some people supporting the student—or maybe even the student himself—decided the idea might be necessary to ensure a free appropriate public education, so they called an IEP meeting. All the people in the meeting are going to discuss whether I should become an accommodation. They'll sit down and decide if I'm absolutely necessary. If I am, then I'll become an accommodation. If I'm not, then I'll just stay an idea. But this doesn't mean a student can't use me; it just means a student doesn't need me.

(singing)
I'm just a function.
Yes, I'm only a function,
and I got as far as the IEP table.
Well, now I'm stuck in committee,
and I'll sit here and wait,
while all the necessary stakeholders discuss and debate
whether they should let me be an accommodation.
How I hope and pray that they will,
but today, I am still just a function.

Boy: Listen to those stakeholders arguing! Is all that discussion and debate about you?

Function: Yeah, and I'm one of the lucky ones. Most ideas never even get this far. I hope they decide to give me good marks; otherwise, I may never become an accommodation.

Boy: Well, if you're not included in an IEP, what's the big deal?

Function: If the IEP committee doesn't include me, I can't protect the student. I can still help him and still be used by him, but no one needs to employ me if they don't want to. Oooh, but it looks like I'm gonna make it! Now they just need to get the tool that makes me available to the student.

Boy: If they decide yes, what happens?

Function: Then the educators need to make sure I'm provided. If the item that provides me is already in the environment, I'm just put in place. If the item that provides me is not already in the environment, then that tool needs to be acquired.

Boy: Oh no!

Function: Oh yes!

(singing)
I'm just a function.
Yes, I'm only a function.
And if they decide on me at the IEP table,
well, then I'm put in place

where I'll be used
just like a lot of other functions
for the student to use.
And if he uses me, then I'll be helping him out.
How I hope and pray that he will,
but today, I am still just a function.

Boy: You mean, even if the adults on the IEP team say you should be an accommodation, the student can still say no?

Function: Yes, that's called a veto. No student is forced to use any tool. If the student vetoes me, I have to go back to the IEP meeting, where they'll discuss me again. But by that time, you're so old they'll probably consider a different function...

Boy: By that time, it's very unlikely that you'd be helping the student anymore. It's not easy to become an accommodation, is it?

Function: Maybe!

(singing)
But how I hope and I pray that I will.
But today, I am still just a function.

Educator: They adopted you, Function! Now you're an accommodation!

Function: Oh yes!!!

(Note: In case you're unfamiliar with *Schoolhouse Rock!*, here's a link to watch the original that inspired this example, "I'm Just a Bill": bit.ly/howabillbecomesalaw.)

The Least Restrictive Option

The number of potential solutions that could be applied to help a student achieve any given goal is vast. Should you apply option A, option B, option C, some combination of them all, or heck, maybe it should be option Z? Each method, strategy, and/or tool a team might employ could work to assist the student, so how does a team decide what to try first?

Individual team members might have a different idea as to which option would work best for the student. *Best*, however, is a relative term. Furthermore, nowhere in the law is the word *best* referenced in relation to the selection, acquisition, and implementation of technology. *Best schmest!* A term that is referenced in the law is *least restrictive environment.*

A least restrictive environment is defined this way by the Individuals with Disabilities Education Improvement Act (PL 108-446): "To the maximum extent appropriate, children with disabilities, including children in public or private institutions or other care facilities, are educated with children who are not disabled, and special classes, separate schooling, or other removal of children with disabilities from the regular educational environment occurs only when the nature or severity of the disability of a child is such that education in regular classes, with the use of supplementary aids and services, cannot be achieved satisfactorily."

According to what is outlined in the law, what is best for a student is the path that restricts that student the least. The term *least restrictive environment* is usually referenced in relation to the physical space and the type of program in which the student will be involved, but it can also be used to reference the types of tools that will be used.

Could the definition be revised to include technology?: "To the maximum extent appropriate, children with disabilities ... are educated *using the same technology as* children who are not disabled, and ... other removal of *or application of special technologies for* children with disabilities from the regular educational environment occurs only when the nature or severity of the disability of a child is such that education in regular classes, with the use of supplementary aids and services, cannot be achieved satisfactorily *using the technology available in the environment.*" The inclusive intent of the law fits with the selection and application of technology, as well as the physical location and service delivery model.

When an IEP team is attempting to decide which option to apply for a student, that team should ask itself the following question: "Of all the options, which is the least restrictive?"

Whether making decisions at an IEP meeting, planning an educational experience, or working on the fly in a teachable moment with a student, choose the least restrictive option. With conscious effort, in time, the process of considering what is least restrictive will become easier and more innate (if it wasn't already so). And you, your colleagues, and your students will all reap the benefits. You'll be able to rest assured that the technology you've selected for a student is only going to unlock doors and provide opportunities for his or her success.

SETTLE

Educational experience designers can use an expanded version of the SETT Framework to determine what technology or adjustments should be made to support a student by considering the addition of an "L" for "least restrictive option" and an "E" for "everyone" to the acronym. Beyond examining the student, environments, tasks, and tools, the least restrictive option(s) might also be considered. And over time, educational experience designers can use cumulative data across a variety of students to make decisions about what technologies are worthy of consideration for mass implementation to mass populations of students. (This concept is further examined in chapter 10.)

Foregoing the Technology Continuum

Once upon a time, educators working in assistive technology considered tools on a continuum from low tech (or light tech) to high tech. Folding pieces of paper to make a graphic organizer might be on the low-tech end of the spectrum, while using a piece of software to provide structure to a piece of writing would be considered high tech. Using a pacing board or a picture exchange system would be considered a low-tech method of facilitating communication, while using a digital touch-screen voice-output device would be considered high tech.

Educators used the continuum to guide decisions about the order in which technology should be applied. Many (this author included) believed no-tech and low-tech options should be implemented and attempted first, before considering a more high-tech intervention. In the past, many low-tech items were more portable, more immediately available (and, coincidentally, more cost effective), and could be used more ubiquitously. Repairing and replacing a low-tech device often took less time than a high-tech item that needed to be fixed. If a student's problem could be addressed with something low tech, this was considered generally less restrictive than something high tech.

Although these categories still exist, the idea that no tech or low tech should be applied before high tech has changed. In contemporary education and society, carrying and wearing high-tech devices is commonplace. The ubiquity of high-tech devices no longer makes them less restrictive than carrying a paper-based support. In fact, as the use of paper becomes more obsolete, it is not a stretch to think that paper could be considered more restrictive. Rather than following a no-tech to high-tech continuum, make decisions based on what might be considered least restrictive.

TO ERR IS HUMAN

No matter your role, chances are you're going to make a mistake somewhere down the line. Maybe you should have provided more or less assistance in a given situation. Looking back, maybe intervention B should have been implemented instead of intervention A. Second-guessing and making mistakes is part of the human condition.

If mistakes are inevitable, what can we do to mitigate their negative impact? Err on the side of believing in people. Err on the side of having expectations that are too high, not too low. Err on the side of attempting to choose the action that is least restrictive.

Least-Restrictive-Option Practice Scenarios

What follows is a series of common scenarios in which the IEP team is requesting assistance in the selection of technology for a student. Whatever your role, ask yourself which would be the least restrictive option. And don't feel limited to the multiple-choice responses. Maybe an option of your own making would be considered least restrictive.

Scenario 1—Production of Text

A student without a diagnosis that impacts motor function is having difficulty producing thoughts in a written format. The student demonstrates the ability to express himself verbally. The student is working on projects and, at times, based on the product he'd like to share with the public, needs the ability to produce text in a written format using appropriate syntax and grammar. To help this student learn how to produce text, which option would be considered least restrictive?

    a.   Dictating to another person who scribes for him.

    b.   Dictating to devices that scribe for him.

    c.   Recording audio into a graphic organizing template and then listening to these audio files while typing in what was previously recorded.

    d.   Some combination of any or all the above.

Dictation to a human scribe is limiting because the student is relying on another person; the student is not practicing acquisition of a skill to improve his own functionality. Despite the increasing accuracy of speech-to-text software, depending on the background noise of the recording environment, clarity of speech, and clarity of thought, efficient use of speech-to-text is still a skill that needs to be learned. Further, for every minute the student is practicing using his voice to produce text, he is not practicing the building of motor plans to access the keyboard.

In the student's future, will there be instances where it will not be appropriate to produce text using one's voice? What if the student needs to take notes when a teacher is talking to a classroom of other students? As an adult in the future, what if the student is in a professional-development workshop and would like to take notes while his coworkers are sitting near him? In each of these scenarios, is it practical to produce text using speech or would it be more practical to produce text silently by using a keyboard?

By recording audio, listening to it, and building the motor plans necessary to become a proficient user of a keyboard, the student is relying on his strength of verbal expression and spending his time learning a lifelong skill. Practicing keyboarding does not, however, preclude one from using speech-to-text in certain situations. Perhaps both methods can be practiced depending on the circumstances. Perhaps in school, the student practices recording audio, playing it back, and accessing the keyboarding because the noisy environment makes speech-to-text less conducive; but at home, in the car, or in some other quiet environment, the student uses speech-to-text. For this scenario, perhaps the least restrictive option is implementation of multiple tools used at select times.

Scenario 2—Motor Access to a Keyboard

A student in first grade would like to write a thank-you note to an author for creating his favorite book series. The student is learning how to compose sentences, but his fine-motor control currently impacts his ability to accurately target the keys on a keyboard. Those developing his Individualized Education Program have devised a long-term goal for the student to become a functional user of a keyboard, and those designing his educational experiences have planned opportunities to practice writing by accessing the keyboard.

The student accurately presses the target key approximately 85 percent of the time. Approximately 5 percent of the mishits are due to holding the key down too long. His palm or other parts of his hand accidentally pressing other keys make up the remaining 10 percent of the mishits. The student attempts to self-correct, noticing most of his mishits. What might be the least restrictive option to help this student?

a. Provide a larger keyboard so he has more surface area to target each key.

b. Provide access to word prediction so he has fewer keystrokes.

c. Make physical adjustments to the keyboard, such as altering the angle or providing a wrist rest.

d. Provide auditory feedback so he hears every letter spoken aloud as he types.

e. Use accessibility features of the operating system to adjust how much time it takes to hold down a key before it repeats.

f. Place stickers on some of the keys to make the letters easier to see.

g. Turn off the real-time grammar-and-spelling function to encourage the student to ignore the mishits and correct them during an editing phase of the writing process.

h. Some combination of any or all the above.

Use of any keyboard other than a typical QWERTY keyboard should be considered with great caution. Learning to keyboard involves the building of motor memory, which takes time and practice. Changing the size of the keyboard might delay the learning of motor patterns necessary to ensure proficiency. Research suggests that word prediction shows promise in decreasing spelling and typographical errors but has little to no effect on increasing the speed at which someone types (Mezei & Heller, 2009). Therefore, although word prediction might help the student decrease the overall number of keystrokes it takes to enter a word, it is not likely that word prediction would help this student improve his typing abilities. The percentage of accuracy would be consistent no matter how many keystrokes there are. Having the opportunity to press fewer keys might increase how long it takes to learn the motor patterns associated with learning the skill of keyboarding.

The student is already identifying errors he is making; therefore, it likely unnecessary for the student to hear each letter aloud or to see the errors in real time as he presses them. Using a typical QWERTY keyboard, the least restrictive option for the student might be making physical adjustments to the keyboard position and adjusting the accessibility features, such as turning on and setting a "filter keys" function to ignore brief or repeated keystrokes.

It is unclear whether visual processing is impacting the student's ability to target and press the appropriate keys. Placing stickers on certain letters such as the vowels might also help the student target appropriate keys without restricting the student's current or future abilities in any way. Learning to edit and revise during a separate editing phase is another lifelong skill worthy of practice.

Scenario 3—Access to a Computing Device

Every student in the class has access to a computing device with internet capabilities. Some bring their own devices, but for those who don't (for whatever the reason), the school has devices available as loaners. One student in the class has trouble accessing devices due to his current fine-motor abilities. In general, which is the least restrictive user interface to help this student access the internet?

   a.   A one-button mouse

   b.   A two-button mouse

   c.   A trackpad

   d.   A touchscreen

   e.   A joystick

   f.   A trackball

g. A switch or multiple switches

h. Voice control

i. Depends on the nature of the student's fine-motor abilities

j. Depends on the nature of the technology available in the classroom

Although the final decision may depend on the student's fine-motor abilities, there may be a general continuum to follow when considering access. At one point in history, the primary user interface with a computer relied on a person's control of a mouse. Trackpads delivered another mainstream, built-in option for interfacing with computers, and touchscreens were optional peripherals that could be placed over monitors and used to help people who had difficulties accessing the mouse. Now, one of the primary interfaces with computing devices is a touchscreen.

When considering how any user will interface with computing devices, use a continuum starting with what might be the most widely used interface to the least widely used. Perhaps this continuum is as follows: touchscreen, trackpad, two-button mouse (depending on the device), one-button mouse, trackball/joystick, a switch or multiple switches, voice control. It should be noted that with advancements in artificial intelligence and voice-controlled devices (Amazon Echo, Siri on iOS devices, Google Home, Cortana, etc.), one might consider voice control earlier on the continuum.

The question of defining a continuum based on what is least restrictive is always in flux and up for debate. Although a team might consider what is already available in the classroom, this should not be a limiting factor. If a student requires an access methodology to maintain a free appropriate public education, then required technology should be acquired and made available to the student.

Scenario 4—Early Language Development

A student is not yet using verbal speech as his primary form of expression by the age of three. He primarily gestures and makes vocalizations to gain attention, make requests, and protest. He attends an early-childhood special-education classroom comprised of students with and without disabilities. The IEP team is considering the implementation of a device that might help him communicate. Which of the following is the least restrictive option to help this student learn language and express himself?

   a.   Use of a static, paper-based board comprised of 8–12 words with symbols.

   b.   Use of a static, paper-based board comprised of approximately 80 words with symbols.

   c.   Use of a static voice-output device comprised of 8–12 words with symbols.

   d.   Use of a static voice-output device comprised of approximately 80–100 words with symbols.

   e.   Use of a dynamic voice-output device with a complete language system and access to thousands of words with symbols.

   f.   Some combination of any or all the above.

From the moment a baby is born (and perhaps even before), the child is immersed in a language-rich environment. The baby is exposed to words constantly, whether being spoken to directly or experiencing words that people use in the baby's presence. After months of exposure, if the baby maintains the ability to learn and express language verbally, verbal speech will emerge and eventually become her or his primary form of expression.

A person with a language delay or a person who, for whatever reason, never uses verbal speech as her or his primary form of verbal expression, requires exposure to language using the methodology he or she will be using to generate language as soon as possible. This strategy is called "aided language stimulation" or "aided language input."

When implementing an augmentative or alternative communication system with a student, the sooner you can begin teaching and modeling on a robust language system, the better. Perhaps what is least restrictive is the implementation of a dynamic voice-output device built as an entire language system, with immediate access to thousands of words and symbols, and working in conjunction with communication partners (perhaps on a second device) who use the system to model expressive language with early syntactic structures, such as pronoun + verb ("you go"), pronoun + qualifier ("it big"), and subject + verb + object ("I like it").

Implementation of a static, paper-based board matching the home screen (of most frequently used words) could also be implemented with all the students in the classroom that don't require a voice-output device. Modeling the location of vocabulary through the usage of a language system offers a visual way to learn language structures for the other students while also increasing the exposure for the student learning to use the device.

Scenario 5—Summative Assessment Selection

You've volunteered to sit on the selection committee charged with the task of purchasing a new summative assessment tool for all fourth graders. The committee has already established that the assessment will be given on computers and is entertaining different options from various vendors. Approximately 15 percent of the students in fourth grade have an accommodation guaranteeing them access to text-to-speech functionality when accessing text during instruction and during most testing.

Your school district maintains a license to robust literacy software, which provides text-to-speech support when accessing any browser and when accessing word-processing files. Any student in your district, with or without a disability, has access to text-to-speech. When considering which assessment to purchase, which functionality for text-to-speech provides the least restrictive option?

   a.   Assessment software built with its own text-to-speech function.

   b.   Assessment software built to utilize the text-to-speech function of the specific literacy software your school district is already using.

   c.   Assessment software built to utilize any text-to-speech function of any software.

   d.   Some combination of any or all the above.

Have you ever rented a car? When someone rents a car, the driver typically takes a few moments to figure out where the controls are located and how they work. After this period of orientation, the driver pulls away and begins the journey. When it starts to rain, while driving in slick and dangerous conditions, the driver might be forced to hunt for the controls for the windshield wipers. In one's own car, where the driver is intimately familiar with the location and functionality of the controls, there is no hunting. Even though the functionality exists in both vehicles, using a familiar automobile speeds up the journey, increases the comfort level, and decreases distractibility. (Keep your eyes on the road, mister!)

When considering which assessment software to purchase, perhaps the least restrictive option is to select the software built to utilize any text-to-speech function of any software. Although in this case, your school district provides literacy-support software, and most students might be familiar with that functionality, not every student may be using that software to access the text-to-speech function.

For example, despite the district having purchased the Read&Write for Windows and Read&Write for Google Chrome extension, both of which provide a text-to-speech function, some students might be more familiar with or more comfortable using a different tool that also provides text-to-speech, such as the ChromeVox extension or the screen-reading tools built into the operating system of their own device, which they have been using in school.

During the assessment, if it is at all possible, providing students access to the text-to-speech function using the same tool and techniques they have been using all year long increases their comfort level, decreases confusion, and helps ensure what is being measured is not impacted by unfamiliarity with the tool.

Scenario 6—Which Words?

A student is four years old and not using verbal expression as her primary form of communication. The IEP team has implemented an augmentative communication device and is attempting to teach the student how to use it by modeling with the same device, planning immersive experiences that expose her to specific words and following a least-to-most prompting hierarchy to give the student the greatest chance possible to use the words on the device (Finke et al., 2017). According to the Global Language Monitor (bit.ly/glmnumberofwords), there are over one million words in the English language. With so many words to learn, which words or groups of words would be considered the least restrictive option to teach?

a. Expose the student to the greatest number of nouns possible.

b. Expose the student to the greatest number of verbs possible.

c. Expose the student to the greatest number of adjectives possible.

    d.   Expose the student to the greatest number of prepositions possible.

    e.   Expose the student to the greatest number of adverbs possible.

    f.   Expose the student to all parts of speech equally.

    g.   A combination of any or all the above.

The amount of time any educator has with a student is finite, but the amount a student can learn is infinite. When attempting to teach language to any student, the educational experience designer focuses the student's experience on vocabulary that will restrict the student in the least way possible. When it comes to teaching language to a student who is learning to use an augmentative device, which words the student is exposed to and practices is significant. Choosing the least restrictive vocabulary is an important factor in determining a student's future ability to communicate using language.

Research suggests that most of the words people say in any given context at any given point in their lives, regardless of the language, is made up of approximately the same 300 to 350 words (Baker, Hill, & Devylder, 2000). These 300 to 350 most frequently used words are known as core vocabulary and appear to be consistently used by everyone. In fact, these 300 to 350 words make up approximately 80 percent of what any given person says if she or he primarily uses speech to communicate. These words are mostly verbs, adjectives, pronouns, prepositions (*in, out, over, under,* etc.), and demonstratives (*this, that, these, those,* etc.). Nouns are the part of speech that makes up most of the known words, but statistically, are used the least frequently. For example, although you likely know the words *sasquatch, leprechaun, zombie, pirate,* and *hippopotamus,* those words are very rarely used in daily conversation. Nouns only make up approximately 20 percent of the words spoken in any given conversation.

Following a pattern of typical language development would mean designing experiences in which the student is focused on learning how to use core vocabulary words approximately 80 percent of the time and noncore vocabulary words (known as "fringe vocabulary words") the other 20 percent of the time. Providing experiences for the student to learn how to use and combine the most frequently used words into sentences gives the student the greatest bang for her buck and would be, perhaps, the least restrictive.

Scenario 7—Agendas with a Bite

The local orthodontist has approached your middle school and generously offered to provide agenda books for every student. Agenda books are paper-based notebooks with a calendar and inspirational quotes along the margins. This works for the orthodontist because the name of her company is placed somewhere every student in the local school district will be exposed to daily. The orthodontist also thinks that many parents will be reviewing the agenda books on a nightly (or at least weekly) basis, which might plant the seed of the company name in the brains of the family members who pay the bills.

The orthodontist isn't some scheming, seedy monster trying to exploit students for her own gains. Instead, she thinks agenda books are something every student in school needs. After all, she used an agenda book to keep herself organized when she was in school, and now, she's an orthodontist! She sincerely wants to contribute and thinks that providing an agenda book for each student would be a win for her, a win for the school, and a win for the students. To her, it's a win-win-win scenario! Which of these is the least restrictive option?

    a. Accept the agenda books from the orthodontist for every student.

    b. Invite the orthodontist to provide the agenda books for a percentage of students.

    c. Invite the orthodontist to sponsor something other than the agenda books.

    d. Decline the offer for agenda books.

    e. Some combination of any of the above.

They're *free* agenda books! *Yo! Woot! Free stuff!* Free stuff is always good, right? *Gimme! Gimme! Gimme!*

In reality, agenda books are a legacy tool from what is rapidly becoming a bygone era in education. The books themselves are wrought with problems. Legible handwriting, remembering to bring the book home, locating the book, transporting the book, remembering to review what has been written in the book, protecting the book from wear and tear, and generally keeping the book in one piece are just some of the issues making this tool a restrictive option.

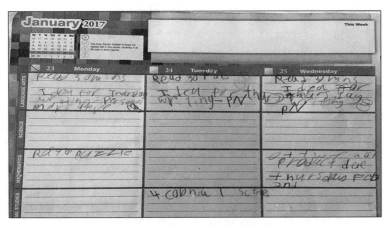

Figure 5.1 A sample page of a middle school agenda book.

An alternative option is to use a student's personal device or a school-provisioned device in conjunction with an online calendar system. Students lose or misplace their personal devices less frequently than they do agenda books; and when they do lose them, most devices can be tracked geographically, making them easier to find.

An online calendar system eliminates legibility concerns and offers multiple modalities for data entry on multiple devices from multiple locations. The student can use different digital functions, such as word prediction and spell check, to expressively enter the information and has access to other functions, such as text-to-speech, to review this information.

Information in an online calendar is typically searchable, which allows a student to more readily find whatever information he or she is looking for. And online calendars are shareable. A user's calendar can be shared with family members, educators, and friends, and can be set up in such a way that those with access can see each other's events.

Online calendars can also be a source of data collection, where educators can review progress on goals related to executive functioning. For instance, educators can see how often a student enters in appropriate dates for task completion and compare that to when the tasks are expected to be completed. If the student has set dates for completing different stages of a project, an educator, parent, or any other support person can compare target dates with completion dates.

Online calendars also include a reminder functionality that might provide some sort of notifications to help the user remember what needs to be accomplished and when. Since agenda books are generally less accessible than an online calendar, an online calendar typically makes for a less restrictive option.

However, there might be some students who are successfully using an agenda book and who, for whatever reason, prefer to use an agenda book to keep organized. Perhaps for these students, the agenda book is the least restrictive option. These students should have access to the tool that makes sense to them but also have the option to switch to another tool.

Regarding the orthodontist, perhaps the least restrictive option would be to accept the donation of a very limited number of agenda books for the few students who want them and also present the orthodontist with an invitation to sponsor some other school event or initiative.

Scenario 8—Prompting in Language Instruction for a User of AAC

You're part of a team that has decided a student requires an augmentative/alternative communication (AAC) device to learn language. The team knows that placing a device without also having a plan for how to teach language with it would likely result in minimal or negligible progress. So, the team develops a plan, attempting to provide opportunities to learn language all day long. Learning to use language with others necessitates that another person be present. The communication partner teaches the language by providing direct instruction and prompting. Prompting can come in a variety of forms. Which type of prompting is least restrictive?

a. Provide as many prompts as possible.

b. Provide as few prompts as possible.

c. Maintain a hierarchy of prompts, going from the least to the most direct type of prompts as deemed necessary by the communication partner.

d. Maintain a hierarchy of prompts, going from the most to the least direct type of prompts as deemed necessary by the communication partner.

e. Some combination of any or all the above.

Research suggests that implementing and maintaining a least-to-most prompting hierarchy helps the student learn language using a communication device (Finke et al., 2017). Although techniques and types of prompts may vary from clinician to clinician and among research studies, a least-to-most prompting hierarchy follows a consistent, systematic progression. Doing so maximizes the opportunities for a student to demonstrate independent use of the aspect of language being learned.

The least direct type of prompting might be to wait expectantly for a communication partner to respond to an utterance. If the student does not respond, looking at the student quizzically or shrugging might be the next least direct prompt. If the student still does not respond, the next prompt might be to ask a guiding question, such as "Well?" or "What's next?" Follow with "Your turn" or "You do it" if necessary. If the student continues to be unresponsive, then it might be time to point to the AAC device and give direct instruction, like "Press these." If that doesn't elicit a response, then the communication partner might press some of the words for the student, completing the entire phrase for the student if he or she has yet to respond. The most direct type of modeling might be to use a hand-over-hand technique on the device that guides the student to the words necessary to complete a response. Using a least-to-most hierarchy also ensures the team working with the student is providing the least restrictive approach to language instruction.

Scenario 9—The Student Who Was Too Low to Learn Language

You are working on a team at the high school level to develop supports for a student who has a rare genetic disorder that impacts cognition, language, and motor function. Due to a combination of seizure activity and required medicinal support, the student is often lethargic at school and falls asleep in his wheelchair frequently. Past teams working with the student have implemented single-switch voice-output devices that say whole word phrases, such as "Good morning, everyone" and "I want more, please." The student uses a gross-motor swiping motion to press the switch when it is placed on a tray in front of him. The new team is determining which communication supports are required to ensure this student receives a free appropriate public education. Regarding the use of an augmentative communication system, which is the least restrictive option?

    a. The student is "too low" to learn language (for example, to express himself using multiple combinations of words).

b. The student is capable of learning language (for example, if only he had proper access and educational experiences, he could someday learn to express himself using multiple combinations of words).

Although it might be an entirely true statement that even given appropriate tools and strategies, with the most experienced clinicians and educators working with augmentative communication, the student might not ever learn to combine multiple words into phrases or sentences, that doesn't mean not to try. Which person do you want to be—the person who believes the student is "too low" to learn language or the person who goes down swinging, giving the student every ounce of opportunity for success?

Denying the student the opportunity to learn language does not ensure a free appropriate public education but *does* ensure that the educators working with him will be correct in their assumption that he will never learn language. Believing the student can and will learn to express himself through language is the least restrictive option. The only student who was ever too low to learn language is the one who wasn't given the opportunity.

Scenario 10—On the Fly

You're an educational experience designer working with students who are collaborating on the creation of a video about stroke prevention. One of the students has an uncle who recently had a stroke. While researching the cause of the stroke, the student began learning about human physiology and how the circulatory system works. The student learned that symptom awareness and early detection can result in a better prognosis. After sharing his research with some of his classmates, they agreed to help him create an informational video and brochure that could be used to raise awareness. As an educational experience designer, what's the least restrictive option?

a. Give a lecture on the circulatory system.

b. Assign a project that requires everyone in the class to write a report on the relationship between the circulatory system and a stroke.

c. Provide suggestions, resources, and feedback to students while they generate the informational video and brochure.

The role of the educational experience designer is to guide student learning. Guidance comes in the form of making suggestions, helping locate and scrutinize resources, providing feedback, and assisting with project management, including the creation of deadlines. Although some direct instruction can be included, it is not a central focus of the project. Filling the role of project manager instead of content provider restricts the student in the least possible way.

Education Before Restriction: Decision-Making with a Bite

Sometimes people grind their teeth in their sleep, increasing the rate of enamel erosion. To prevent this from happening, a dentist might recommend the use of an occlusal guard, a fitted piece of plastic that covers a person's teeth and restricts them from touching. At night, when the grinding occurs, the teeth move against the plastic rather than the enamel of the other teeth, slowing the rate of erosion. (Thank you, dentist!)

Educators take a different approach. An educational experience designer would ask, "What's causing the teeth to be ground in the first place?" and consider ways to teach or train the body or mind to no longer grind the teeth. It might take a little longer to get to why the problem exists, but once identified, a solution can be put in place that addresses the root cause.

When considering the least restrictive option in any given situation, it might occur to someone to restrict a student's access to something. That might mean taking something away, turning something off, or removing something from a situation. But we're educators—we educate. Resist the urge to lead with restriction. Whenever possible, lead with education.

The Fallacy of the One Solution

It is possible—even likely—that there might be more than one solution to any given problem. Centuries of storytelling have conditioned us to think differently, believing that there is only *one* way to do anything. How do you kill Smaug, the fearsome dragon? Shoot an arrow in the missing scale on his belly. How do you blow up the Death Star? Launch a torpedo down a small shaft leading to its core. Most books and movies have only one ending, where our heroes ride a small glimmer of hope to victory.

Back in the land where truth is stranger and more complex than fiction, where the outcome isn't preordained and scripted by writers, educational experience designers have many different options when it comes to technology consideration. There is no singular, set path that brings people to the best solution. The truth is, there might be multiple tools, strategies, and approaches that assist a student to achieve his or her educational goals. There doesn't need to be one way to win the game, as there are almost always *multiple* ways to win. It's a Choose Your Own Adventure novel in a story about student achievement!

Imagine there is a student—let's call him Tucker—who has the goal of writing a cohesive five-paragraph essay. The IEP team agrees that Tucker requires access to a digital graphic organizer and word processing to generate the text. However, the team is unsure whether the function of word prediction is necessary to help him accurately spell words or if a better approach might be for the student to dictate words into the computer, allowing the text to appear on the screen as he types. Both approaches have pros and cons related to implementation, depending on the circumstance. Further complicating the discussion is which name brand of word prediction and/or speech recognition to use.

The team is at an impasse because they are looking for the best solution for Tucker. What they are failing to realize is that, perhaps, there is more than one best solution; maybe multiple solutions will help him achieve the goal. The more time spent on learning a skill increases the likelihood of acquiring that skill.

If the IEP team chooses to focus its efforts on learning keyboarding skills in conjunction with word prediction, Tucker will spend his time on the keyboard using word prediction, and it is likely he will make progress toward the goal of writing cohesive five-paragraph essays. If he spends his time using speech-to-text, then it is likely he will still make progress toward his composition goal. If he uses some combination of these functions in different environments, such as implementing word prediction at school and speech-to-text at home, he is still spending time working on the goal of making him a better writer of five-paragraph essays—tool selection is ancillary to the goal. No matter which tool or combination of tools gets applied, Tucker wins, because he'll be spending time working on his goal.

Measuring Outcomes and the Myth of Causality

You've considered and implemented an intervention for an individual or for a group of individuals. How do you know that what you've implemented is working, making the change you wanted it to make?

The answer is simple: *you don't.*

The idea that one can know—without a shadow of a doubt—that a specific piece of technology, intervention, resource, or support caused an individual to meet a goal is a myth. To analyze the effectiveness of an instructional methodology or technology, educators might attempt to follow a structure based on a version of the scientific method. The scientific method states that one should start with a fundamental statement—a hypothesis—and then make observations to confirm or deny that claim. We often call these observations "data" or "evidence."

IEP teams meet to establish goals for the student to achieve. The generation of a goal acts as the formulation of the hypothesis in the scientific method. For example, if a goal is to generate a five-sentence paragraph using a topic sentence, three details that support the topic sentence, and a conclusion, then the hypothesis is that the tools, strategies, and interventions applied by the IEP team will sufficiently help the student complete that goal.

Throughout the course of the school year, the educational team makes observations that either support or deny this claim. If the student achieves the goal, then the hypothesis is confirmed and the tools, strategies, and interventions are deemed effective in helping the student achieve the goal. If the goal is not achieved, then the educational team analyzes the observations to assess why the goal was not achieved.

Although the process attempts to parallel the scientific method by formulating a hypothesis and then making observations to confirm or deny that hypothesis, the problem is that it is impossible to control the variables in an instructional setting. Furthermore, educators make quantitative and qualitative observations throughout the year, but having these points of information doesn't necessarily prove whether an intervention was the cause—or even a factor—in the achievement of the goal.

Using the same example of assisting a student in his goal of writing a five-sentence paragraph, perhaps the IEP team introduced a graphic organizer along with other strategies, such as direct instruction, verbally recording each sentence, transcribing it once he's listened to it, and then using text-to-speech to play back his work once he's finished it. The graphic organizer also employed a color-coding scheme by which the first cell for the topic sentence is green, the cells for the three details are yellow, and the final cell for the conclusion is red.

Suppose in one year's time the student achieves the goal and successfully demonstrates the ability to write the essay. Which of the interventions was successful? Can any one intervention be isolated as essential? For instance, would the student have performed just as well without the color coding? Would the student have achieved the goal sooner had the graphic organizer been used more often? Perhaps the student became dedicated to achieving the goal because of some extrinsic motivator unknown to the educators, like wanting to emulate a relative who writes as a career?

Likewise, if the student did not achieve the goal, can any one intervention be isolated as having not worked? Variables such as duration, presentation, and engagement all factor into performance and achievement.

There are just too many uncontrollable variables impacting student performance all at once to know for sure that any one of those variables is the cause of the change. So, how can effectiveness be measured?

Although often presumed to be quantitative and numeric, data can also be qualitative and descriptive. Data can come in many modalities (audio, video, images, text) and generated from assessments, projects, endeavors, work samples, and other achievements (Bugaj & Poss, 2016). This structure provides a model for how an educational team can determine if an intervention is working to support a student in achieving a goal: Throughout the course of a year, the educational team working with a student collects evidence on student progress toward a goal. The educational team collects as many individual facts pertaining to the goal as possible, using many different modalities from a wide range of sources. The educational team then analyzes the evidence to draw conclusions about which tools, strategies, and interventions are working to help the student achieve the goals. Next, educators construct a case for or against the continued use of a tool, strategy, or intervention based on the body of evidence. The larger the body of evidence, the easier it becomes for the educational team to make informed decisions about what is working and what is not. Educators use the evidence they've collected and analyzed to weave a tapestry pertaining to effectiveness.

For example, in the case of a student writing a five-sentence paragraph, the educational team might look at all of the evidence collected, such as number of times the graphic organizer was introduced; the topics involved; the authenticity of the assignment; the structure or layout of the graphic organizer; how often the student used the strategy of verbally recording audio prior to text production; sentence length and complexity from the writing samples; how often the student used text-to-speech for editing; as well as anecdotal data from the student made via verbal comments, conversation, or Likert scales that rate the student's perceptions about the use of each tool, strategy, or intervention. Using this entire body of evidence, the educational team collectively determines the effectiveness of each component.

Proving that a singular intervention is the cause of a student's success or that a singular intervention is effective is typically not possible. It isn't necessarily about what the educational team can prove is working but, rather, about what the educational team—including the student—perceives to be working based on the body of evidence. The more evidence an educational team has, the better suited they are to make decisions about future instructional methodologies. Even the data points that do not necessarily fit with the rest of the evidence need to be explored or explained to tell a comprehensive narrative about a student's performance. Accurate conclusions cannot be made without examination of all the evidence. Therefore, it's imperative to collect as much evidence from as many sources as possible to make informed, reasonable decisions.

CHAPTER **6**

The Birth of an Accessible-Design Facilitator

Educational experience designers, just like any other educational professional, have some level of knowledge of what is available to help all students, including those with disabilities. Like every professional working in education, they have developed a bag of tricks pertaining to tools they know how to employ. However, the bag, no matter how large, can never hold the entirety of every trick known to humankind. There's too much research and too many tools and ways to use that research to know everything.

Educational experience designers need partners who can help them learn how to consider, offer, and weave present, emerging, and compelling technologies into the educational experience they are designing—partners who are focused on the needs of people with disabilities and can help keep accessibility in the forefront of the educational experience. Similarly, IEP teams sometimes need assistance in researching and outlining options to consider. No matter their role, educators will likely need support brainstorming through a problem, developing a plan of action, analyzing collected data, or acquiring and implementing items to ensure that the experiences being designed are accessible. Who does your educational agency have available as a resource to provide this needed assistance?

Educational institutions also need assistance facilitating agency-wide change to actively embrace inclusive and accessible practices. Who helps educational institutions create a culture in which inclusivity happens so naturally that people don't need to give it conscious thought?

In this chapter, you'll:

1. Explore the role of a person or team of persons responsible for assisting educational experience designers and IEP teams in the adoption of inclusive and accessible practices, including technology.

2. Learn strategies for how to advocate for the existence of such a person or team of persons who facilitate the infusion of accessible practices at every level throughout the educational agency.

ISTE STANDARDS ADDRESSED

ISTE Standards for Educators 2a. Shape, advance, and accelerate a shared vision for empowered learning with technology by engaging with education stakeholders.

ISTE Standards for Educators 2b. Advocate for equitable access to educational technology, digital content, and learning opportunities to meet the diverse needs of all students.

ISTE Standards for Educators 2c. Model for colleagues the identification, exploration, evaluation, curation, and adoption of new digital resources and tools for learning.

ISTE Standards for Educators 4a. Dedicate planning time to collaborate with colleagues to create authentic learning experiences that leverage technology.

ISTE Standards for Educators 4b. Collaborate and colearn with students to discover and use new digital resources, and diagnose and troubleshoot technology issues.

ISTE Standards for Educators 4c. Use collaborative tools to expand students' authentic, real-world learning experiences by engaging virtually with experts, teams, and students, locally and globally.

ISTE Standards for Educators 4d. Demonstrate cultural competency when communicating with students, parents, and colleagues and interact with them as co-collaborators in student learning.

ISTE Standards for Educators 5a. Use technology to create, adapt, and personalize learning experiences that foster independent learning and accommodate learner differences and needs.

ISTE Standards for Educators 5b. Design authentic learning activities that align with content-area standards, and use digital tools and resources to maximize active, deep learning.

ISTE Standards for Educators 5c. Explore and apply instructional design principles to create innovative digital learning environments that engage and support learning.

ISTE Standards for Educators 6b. Manage the use of technology and student learning strategies in digital platforms, virtual environments, hands-on makerspaces, and/or in the field.

ISTE Standards for Educators 7a. Provide alternative ways for students to demonstrate competency and reflect on their learning by using technology.

A Partner for Improvement

What would be an apt title for an individual whose purpose is to keep abreast of available technology specific to the needs of people with disabilities, and who also brainstorms and collaborates with the educational experience designer to construct accessible, engaging, empowering experiences for all students? What title would match the description of someone who provides assistance to the IEP team when they need help brainstorming potential technology?

For the purposes of this book, let's call the position an:

accessible-design facilitator

An accessible-design facilitator (ADF) has the following responsibilities:

- Coach educational experience designers on how to design inclusive and accessible educational experiences centered on the personalized learning needs of all students, including those with disabilities.

- Facilitate the progression of a decision-making process by an IEP team regarding the evaluation, selection, acquisition, and implementation of technology.

- Assist in the acquisition, distribution, repair, and replacement of technology for students based on decisions outlined within the Individualized Education Program.

- Inform others on the research, technology, and inclusive practices necessary to ensure a free appropriate public education for all students.

- Support other district leaders when new initiatives are proposed to ensure that the initiative is designed with the widest scope of student abilities in mind.

- Serve on committees that make decisions regarding instruction at a district level, including new materials, assessments, or curriculum, to help consider the potential impact on students with disabilities and in other minority populations.

- Educate special-education workers on the contemporary practices and district-wide initiatives occurring in general education to support successful implementation for all students.

- Create, organize, and deliver professional-development opportunities for educators and the community.

- Guide without dictating the actions of others to build up their skill sets.

- Participate on a team with other accessible-design facilitators (depending on the size and nature of your local education agency) to formulate, maintain, and implement district-wide accessibility goals that ensure the development of a culture of inclusivity.

- Analyze district-wide service-delivery data related to technology to help establish future goals and actions (see Figure 6.1).

Figure 6.1 A diagram of support. Accessible-design facilitators have no one central team; instead, they participate on multiple committees and function as team members on a variety of teams.

SETTing Your Focus on the Task

An accessible-design facilitator guides an IEP team through the process of identifying necessary technologies by using the SETT Framework in conjunction with the principle of the least restrictive option. However, the ADF emphasizes analyzing more than just technology needs; the ADF shifts the emphasis by helping an IEP team reconsider and redesign the tasks the student is asked to perform and the environment in which the student is learning.

The accessible-design facilitator works with educational experience designers to design experiences that don't necessarily need modification or adaption. They recognize that what might be a less restrictive way to assist a student is to simply redesign and reconsider the task and the environment rather than provide a tool.

Facilitating = Coaching

An alternative term for accessible-design facilitator might be *accessible-design coach*. The role of the ADF is to coach others through the decision-making process of designing inclusive experiences by representing the available technology. ADFs don't play the game; they help educational experience designers learn how to play the game with the tools, strategies, and techniques at hand.

Coaching is not telling someone what to do but rather an exercise in guidance that takes skill. That skill comes with practice and is learned over time. It is honed and refined through deliberate training (trial and error) with these tools, strategies, and techniques. Beyond knowing something about accessibility, an ADF's goal is to learn how to coach educational experience designers to make the best available, least restrictive decisions to the benefit—and greatness—of the students they support.

AWESOME INSIGHT

An accessible-design facilitator asks in every moment (in every conversation, email, training, or other action), "Am I empowering or am I enabling?"

Justifying the Need for an Accessible-Design Facilitator

If you're reading this right now, you're probably a person who already sees that someone acting in this capacity of an accessible-design facilitator is warranted in your educational agency. It is also entirely possible that you are not the person who can simply slide this position into the budget. You are, however, *the* exact person who can influence the person who is in charge of budgeting. You can use your charm, wit, and winning personality to coax that person into seeing things from your perspective, skillfully demonstrating that the position of accessible-design facilitator is warranted.

When it comes time to make the sales pitch, you'll want to have a deep well of strategies to pull from. Use the following strategies as needed, and of course, don't forget to flash that beautiful smile!

Use the Law and National Initiatives

When advocating for a change in your local educational agency, reference federal policy as evidence for enacting the change. Chapters 2 and 4 mentioned multiple federal laws and national initiatives sanctioned by reputable entities. Use these statutes to lend credence, add validity, and provide rational support for the creation of a position that would help ensure alignment with these doctrines. Demonstrate that the proposed changes to practices aren't just occurring at the whim of a few well-intentioned idealists. It is difficult to dismiss or argue with an existing law or national initiative! Why not use these federal mandates to sway the minds of those who might be resistant to change?

Solve the Right Problem for the Right Person

When you make your pitch, make sure you are solving a problem for the person who is the holder of the purse strings. What are some frequent problems experienced by the person to whom you are making the pitch? Tight budgets, angry community members, costly lawsuits, or anything else that might be plaguing this person might be challenges the new position could solve. Show that an accessible-design facilitator will act like aspirin for whatever headaches she or he is having. Making day-to-day life easier is a very appealing argument for the creation of this position.

Save Money and Time

The accessible-design facilitator will save the educational agency on two of its most precious commodities: time and money. The position is an investment in efficiency, not an expenditure. By having this position in place, time is saved by not having to retrofit poor attempts at initial design. When the ADF provides support to IEP teams, either before or after an IEP meeting, resources are allocated in such a way that could prevent independent educational evaluations (which can be requested by a parent at public expense). Coaching IEP teams through a decision-making process can save time that would otherwise be wasted on considering tools and methodologies already known by the ADF to be ineffective.

In a similar capacity, the accessible-design facilitator can provide advice that prevents an unintended and costly domino effect by serving on committees that make determinations about agency-wide initiatives. It costs less to anticipate the needs of *everyone* in the agency than to make corrections and adaptations once a decision has been made. Further, the accessible-design facilitator can help maintain a system for managing and tracking the inventory acquired by the agency. Keeping accurate records of where equipment exists at any given time decreases the loss of items. This data can also be analyzed and used to anticipate future budgets based on authentic, projected data (versus wild guesses).

Provide Quantitative Data

Numerous data points can be used to make the case for an accessible-design facilitator. Some measurable factors are:

- The number of independent educational evaluations

- The number of accommodations being met with staff rather than technology

- The number of hours it takes to provide an accommodation provided with a staff member rather than technology

- The number of technology purchases that ended up not being implemented by students

- The number of district-wide committees that do not have representation from someone specifically looking at decisions through the lens of accessibility

Data can be used to tell a story that points to the necessity of such a position. The data could also be used as a baseline for setting goals and measuring progress.

Leverage Community Support

Community members and activists can help advocate for change, including the creation of a new position that supports the needs of students. As allies, community members can mobilize and strike a chord with the officials who have the ability to make a change. Parents, relatives, and other members of the community can become champions of change. Whether schools are publicly or privately funded, the people of the community are ultimately paying the bills. Their voices carry weight, and that weight can be heavy. When the community steps on the scale, the needle moves.

Keep Up With (or Ahead of) the Joneses

Do other nearby districts have an accessible-design facilitator or several? If so, use this fact as leverage to persuade the powers that be. If not, your institution could be pioneers in the field, acting as trendsetters for the rest to follow. Your district could be the model others look to for guidance. Your district could lead the way. (Appeals to the ego and bravado can sway those who are reluctant to fund the new position.)

Pull on the Heartstrings

At the center of the argument for an accessible-design facilitator position or positions is the desire to support students. It reminds people who might not get out to see the faces of the students that their decisions have an impact. Their choices have consequences.

To demonstrate the outcomes of the decisions being made, share stories of how these decisions directly and indirectly impact the daily lives of students and the educators who support them. Share stories using multiple modalities, including video, slideshows, written narratives, images, and more. Illuminate the positives, where these decisions worked to help a student and even change a life! These stories can also highlight where the system and the engine that drives it has sputtered, stalled, and ultimately failed.

Construct an alternative ending that inserts an accessible-design facilitator into the plot. Lay out how the ADF changes the narrative from tragedy to triumph. Then ask, "Which story do you want to tell: the story where students continue to live in a world that is not accessible to them or the story of a world where you made the difference by funding the position?"

What a Great Idea You Came Up With!

When you make the pitch, bring up questions that lead the person in charge to come up with the solution of generating the position. Each of the previously listed strategies can be utilized by asking open-ended yet leading questions. For example, "The Every Student Succeeds Act specifically mentions accessibility. What steps are we going to take to make our educational agency more accessible? Who can educators turn to when they need support in designing their lessons?"

As the conversation continues, keep asking questions that guide this person toward the creation of the position: "I like your idea to have educators working in small groups during a professional-development day to make authentic lessons more accessible. How could we keep that learning going beyond just that day? How do we sustain the change? To whom can educators turn to help them design all their lessons all year long?" Then, agree vehemently with the person when she or he says, "What if there were a person who specifically had a job to help educators design more accessible lessons?"

What's the Story with Inventory?

As educators and IEP teams make decisions about which technology to put in place, items will fall into one of two categories: items that are already in the educational environment or items that are not. When a student requires a tool that does not already exist in the environment, that tool needs to be acquired. The accessible-design facilitator can assist with the process of acquiring, maintaining, repairing, and replacing inventory. And as students transfer, the accessible-design facilitator can manage the leftover inventory to reduce loss, waste, and excess.

It is helpful to use some sort of system for tracking this inventory. Items should be cataloged within a database and then tracked by status, such as "available for checkout," "out with a teacher," "out with a student," or "out for repair." When deciding how to best manage this inventory, consider the following.

Who Manages Inventory?

Do you already have people who manage and maintain the inventory in your agency? If so, examine who they are, which departments they work in, and the systems they use in their management efforts. Is this system transferable to other departments? If you do not have people who already do this, examine the steps you would need to take to not only implement a management system but train the staff who will be using it.

Does a System Already Exist to Which You Can Hitch Your Wagon?

How does the library manage its inventory? Can that same system be used to manage inventory of technology used by students with IEPs? Could the library manage the inventory? If not the library, how about the instructional-technology services department? How are the computers, interactive whiteboards, projectors, and other pieces of technology managed? Could that system be adopted to manage the items acquired for students receiving special-education services?

Can You Create a DIY Database?

If using an existing database system is not an option, develop your own system. Using a survey tool like Google Forms would allow you to customize the input method while still maintaining access to the backend database. Alternatively, one could learn a database tool, such as Microsoft Access, to develop a robust inventory system. If your educational institution has its own developers, it might be an option to work with them to build a unique, customized inventory solution tailored to integrate with the specific needs of your agency.

How Is All This Stuff Going to Be Stored and Distributed?

Inventory takes space. Locate a home base for equipment that is accessible to those who need to use it. The device depot, in conjunction with a shared, searchable database, might afford an educational agency the opportunity to effectively share resources and save on redundant spending for currently unused, previously acquired equipment. Educators should be aware, however, that the device availability within a depot should not limit a student. If it is determined that a piece of equipment is necessary to ensure a free appropriate public education but that piece of equipment is not currently available for checkout within inventory, acquisition of a device that fulfills that same need is still required.

Can Inventory Go Home with a Student?

Ultimately, it is the responsibility of the IEP team to decide where a student needs access to items at school but still, as a general principle, let these items go home. There isn't a need for any extra documentation when a piece of technology goes home. Most people aren't out to steal from the school, and for those that are, a form isn't going to stop them. The energy spent developing, distributing, and collecting forms for every piece of inventory does not equate to a meaningful return on that time investment. Make the experience of implementing an item at home as easy and as seamless as possible.

How Do You Do Yearly Maintenance?

Things happen. Despite best intentions, stuff goes missing or gets broken. Items might be misplaced or delivered without being accounted for. Equipment might be placed in the wrong location when returned. Items might get dropped, kicked, or thrown. Periodically, it might be necessary to examine every piece of equipment that belongs to the agency to take stock in what exists, what is missing, and what needs repair. This process keeps the database clean and accurate—at its maximum effectiveness.

How Do We Get Rid of This Stuff?

Technology gets outdated. When a piece of technology is no longer useful, consider using the system your agency has in place for removal of items. If the technology was purchased at public expense, the school district will have a protocol to follow for how to purge it, which might include gifting it to charity or selling it at an auction.

Building an Accessible-Design Team

Depending on the size of your educational agency, more than one accessible-design facilitator may be necessary. Perhaps an entire team is necessary to support the educational experience designers in their mission to create accessible experiences. An accessible-design team can work together to provide more assistance to more educators. Many hands make light work!

Some educational agencies already have an established assistive-technology team or program. Sometimes, that is a single individual with some variance of "assistive technology" in his or her job title. In other agencies, a Universal Design for Learning team might exist to help write curriculum or advocate for inclusive practices.

Whether working alone or on a super team of accessibility avengers, build the program upon the principles of accessible design, not necessarily a focus on assistive technology. The powers of your team come from the principles of Personalized

Learning, Universal Design for Learning, Growth Mindset, Project-Based/Problem-Based Learning, the maker movement, bring your own technology, open education, accessible materials, and the least dangerous assumption. Selection, acquisition, and implementation of technology is ancillary to the design elements of the educational experience. Make sure your team doesn't focus its time and energy on adapting poorly designed instruction but, instead, helps people design educational experiences that don't need to be adapted.

If you're on an assistive-technology team, consider the benefits of rebranding as an accessible-design team. Be the accessible-design team that helps with assistive technology, not the assistive-technology team that helps with accessible design.

It's What You Do That Matters

It doesn't matter if you don't really have a job title that reads "educational experience designer" or "accessible-design facilitator." Even if no one calls you by either of these titles or by some variation of them, it doesn't mean you can't act like you have one of these job titles anyway. You can embody the spirit that these job titles invoke.

It's the actions carried out through daily responsibilities that truly make the difference. Regardless of your actual job title, you can make choices as if you were designing or facilitating accessible educational experiences. Walk the walk; talk the talk; be who you know you need to be. Others will follow.

PART III

REQUESTING ASSISTANCE

CHAPTER 7

Getting, Giving, and Using Assistance

Sometimes an educational experience designer (or EED) needs help using technology to craft accessible and inclusive lessons. Sometimes an IEP team needs assistance considering technology that should be implemented to ensure a free appropriate public education. Sometimes an educational institution needs guidance on how to establish and maintain practices for the benefit of every constituent. This assistance can come from a variety of sources including the accessible-design facilitator.

How does one go about requesting assistance? Is it as simple as climbing to the tallest rooftop and yelling, "I need help!" or does the process need to be more sophisticated than that? Let's dive into this chapter to find out.

In this chapter, you'll:

1. Learn who can provide assistance when assistance is needed.

2. Explore a process by which an IEP team requests assistance in the consideration of technology.

3. Examine agency-wide implications for allocating resources to providing assistance.

ISTE STANDARDS ADDRESSED

ISTE Standards for Educators 2a. Shape, advance, and accelerate a shared vision for empowered learning with technology by engaging with education stakeholders.

ISTE Standards for Educators 2b. Advocate for equitable access to educational technology, digital content, and learning opportunities to meet the diverse needs of all students.

ISTE Standards for Educators 2c. Model for colleagues the identification, exploration, evaluation, curation, and adoption of new digital resources and tools for learning.

Who Can Help?

Help for educational experience designers and IEP teams can come from various sources, such as a school psychologist, educational diagnostician, instructional-technology resource teacher, speech-language pathologists, occupational therapists, physical therapists, vision specialists, hearing specialists, other disciplines and educators, accessible-design facilitators, or any combination of professionals. Assistance in considering technology does not need to come from one specific source (like someone with "assistive technology" in her or his job title); instead, it can come from any variety of sources.

When two colleagues have lunch together and the conversation turns to how to best serve a student, both parties are discussing changes to the environments, tasks, and tools that could be made (the SETT framework). When parents talk to friends at a party about what's going on with their child and that friend offers advice about tools to explore or an approach to take, this is helping to identify technology options. Consulting with *anyone* can be considered a form of assessment. The act of analyzing the documentation and corresponding evidence provided for any situation and then brainstorming what a student could use is another form of assessment. A discussion about the merits of implementing any item along with a discussion about adjustments to the task and environment are discussions about assistive technology.

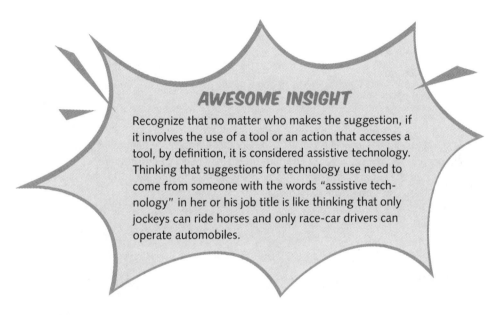

AWESOME INSIGHT

Recognize that no matter who makes the suggestion, if it involves the use of a tool or an action that accesses a tool, by definition, it is considered assistive technology. Thinking that suggestions for technology use need to come from someone with the words "assistive technology" in her or his job title is like thinking that only jockeys can ride horses and only race-car drivers can operate automobiles.

A MATCH GAME!

Let's play a matching game to illustrate who can participate as a member of an IEP team to determine the needs of a student and who can provide support to an IEP team in making this determination. Grab something to draw with (a pencil, pen, marker, crayon, or some annotation tool if you're looking at a digital version).

Look at the two columns shown on the next page, each describing people who are invested in a student's performance. Match the items from the IEP team column to the support column (those who the IEP team might reach out to for support). Take your time as you carefully consider which of the parties in each column can participate in determining what a child with a disability could use to increase, maintain, or improve his or her functional capabilities. (Remember, it's okay to scribble all over this book!)

IEP Team

- Student
- Parent
- Case manager/educational experience designer
- General educator/educational experience designer
- Administrator
- Related service staff
- Advocate

Support

- Friends
- Family
- Other educators
- Accessible-design facilitators
- Community members
- Outside consultants

If the two columns look like you let a toddler loose on a bowl full of wet spaghetti, then you're on the right track. The lines on the page should crisscross repeatedly. *Anyone* in the support column can provide assistance to *anyone* in the IEP column. Good ideas can come from *any* source!

Just Ask! Requesting Assistance Need Not Be Formal

When any member of the IEP team needs assistance considering options, it's appropriate to reach out for help. The request could be initiated informally and not written into the IEP, like when colleagues are just conferring and collaborating. Or the assistance could be a parent asking another parent for advice, an educator asking an accessible-design facilitator for help, or an administrator reaching out to anyone else for advice.

For example, suppose a second-grade student is demonstrating difficulty with spelling. It seems that most words he attempts to spell are done using his memory and not phonemically. The members of his IEP team have implemented various strategies to increase his spelling accuracy, including explicit reading instruction using a multisensory approach, with tools and strategies such as Elkonin boxes, breaking down words into component sounds (using a sing-song voice), playing rhyming games, and accessing a leveled web-based application that targets specific phonemic patterns. However, after two quarters of consistent practice, the student has yet to make sufficient progress toward his goal.

So, the educational experience designer contacts her accessible-design facilitator. Together, they brainstorm research-based intervention options, like the use of word prediction; turning on the captions while watching videos; selecting reading materials of high interest; using kinesthetic, gross-motor activities to walk out the letters of sounds; using gross-motor activities on the interactive whiteboard; standing while working on existing activities; and using a consistent graphic organizer like the Frayer model to teach the meanings of words (Frayer, Frederick, & Klausmeier, 1969). The educational experience designer then begins to implement these strategies when constructing the lessons of the day.

The accessible-design facilitator documents the suggestions in an email to the EED, who, in turn, shares the options with the IEP team. Using existing observable and documented data along with its members' experience, the IEP team makes decisions about which of the options are necessary to guarantee a free appropriate public education. The new interventions, in conjunction with the old, continue to be implemented, and performance continues to be measured.

In this ideal example, the request for assistance and the ideas generated did not originate through any formal request. The educational experience designer simply asked for help, and the help was provided.

AWESOME INSIGHT

In the previous example, the professional contacted by the educational experience designer was the accessible-design facilitator. It could easily have been the occupational therapist, speech-language pathologist, an instructional-technology facilitator, or anyone else capable of brainstorming and researching strategies about how to improve spelling.

Requesting Assistance Prior to an IEP Meeting

IEP team members working with students analyze the performance of a student to decide what actions to take. When educators review data collected on the goals of the IEP, and the analysis of that data shows that the student is demonstrating difficulty achieving that goal, it might be appropriate to ask someone for help. Asking for help can be a decision driven by data.

However, one doesn't necessarily need to analyze the data to know when a student is demonstrating difficulty. Concerns can arise for a variety of reasons, and any IEP team member can ask for assistance at any time prior to or during an IEP meeting. Asking for help prior to an IEP has advantages—one can arrive at the meeting with the options and ideas generated from that discussion, which saves time for the student, as the strategies can be implemented in a more timely fashion. This also results in one less meeting for the IEP team. If the request for help comes at the IEP meeting, then a second IEP meeting needs to be scheduled to review the options and ideas generated from that discussion.

Consider the next two scenarios. Which would you rather see happen?

Scenario 1

The educational experience designer is reflecting on the results of multiple experiences her students have had over the last several weeks. Through reflection, she suspects that despite having access to numerous tools in the environment, and despite the accommodations outlined in the IEP to ensure this access, one of her students, who has a goal of composing a five-paragraph essay, is demonstrating continued difficulty composing thoughts to express himself through writing.

The educational experience designer asks the case manager if the data being collected on this goal bears out her suspicions. Together, the case manager and the EED analyze the data collected as well as the student's work samples, and they conclude that, in fact, the student is demonstrating difficulty. They brainstorm interventions together but wonder about other technologies that could be used to assist this student.

The case manager writes an email to the building's accessible-design facilitator and the instructional-technology resource teacher, asking both for assistance. As soon as possible, all the educators meet to discuss the student, and a list of ideas is generated, including the addition of pictures to graphic organizers for use as prompts, turning off real-time grammar and spell-check to minimize distractions when generating sentences, and inviting the student to voice-record his thoughts rather than writing them. These strategies utilize features of technology already existing in the student's environment.

The next day, the educational experience designer introduces these ideas not only to this student but to the entire class, and the student begins to implement the new strategies. Over the next several weeks, the data collected on this student's ability to compose thoughts through writing shows improvement. An IEP meeting is called to discuss whether these new strategies should be written as accommodations.

Scenario 2

All the members of the IEP team are gathered in a conference room and begin a review of a student's proposed plan. When the conversation turns to goals and what is needed for the student to meet those goals, the parents state that they are concerned about the student's ability to compose five-paragraph essays on various topics. They ask if any additional technology could be used to help with the act of composition, and the school's team members explain that a request for assistance can be written into the IEP. The request for the case manager to meet with an accessible-design facilitator is documented, including a statement about when the IEP team will reconvene to discuss the results of that meeting.

Following the IEP meeting, the case manager contacts the accessible-design facilitator to schedule a meeting to fulfill the request. As soon as possible, all the educators meet to discuss the student and generate a list of ideas, including the addition of pictures to graphic organizers for use as prompts, turning off real-time grammar and spell-check to minimize distractions when generating sentences, and inviting the student to voice-record his thoughts rather than writing them. These strategies utilize features of technology that already exist in the student's environment, which the accessible-design facilitator details in a document. Soon after, the educational experience designer introduces these ideas not only to the student but to the entire class, and the student begins to implement the new strategies.

The IEP team reconvenes by the date determined during the first meeting to discuss this document and whether these new strategies should be written as accommodations.

Scenario 1 versus Scenario 2

In both scenarios, the individual student and the larger body of students benefit from the conference between the case manager and the accessible-design facilitator. However, in the first scenario, the strategies are put in place more expeditiously and with less paperwork. The cost in hours to the educational agency is minimized. Further, in the first scenario, the educators have taken a proactive role in analyzing the data and implementing corrective actions. In the second scenario, the educators are responding reactively to the concerns brought up by the parents. In both scenarios, everyone wins, but in scenario 1, the winning takes place a little bit sooner and with a little less energy.

Eliminate Barriers to Requesting Assistance

Some people hate paperwork and forms. Filling out an intake form, no matter how easy, can act as a barrier to someone requesting assistance. The process should be welcoming, not daunting. The first step in requesting assistance should be to reach out to a person rather than interacting with a form.

If you are attempting to be as accessible to people's needs as possible, then scratch the form and invite people to contact you via email, phone, or another means— especially if the information contained in the form can easily be found elsewhere, like on a student's IEP. Any necessary information that is not already documented can be collected via conversations and discussions with those asking for assistance. Making the first step in obtaining assistance more inviting than the impersonal nature of a form sends a message that the overall experience will be friendly, worthwhile, and collaborative.

It's important to note that not having a form to request assistance does not mean that documentation should not exist. Once assistance is requested, the person receiving the request should document the request, but this could be as simple as an online form that feeds a database about the location and nature of the request.

(*Note:* the responsibility of entering that data into the database falls to the person who is receiving the request, not the one making it.)

Taking the time to collect and then analyze this data later can produce insights into trends, helping to shape goals while generating the necessary evidence to make alterations to action plans regarding how best to provide assistance.

Requesting Assistance During an IEP Meeting

According to federal law, an assistive technology service is defined as "any service that directly assists a child with a disability in the selection, acquisition, or use of an assistive technology device," which includes the evaluation of the needs of the child and a functional evaluation of the child's needs in his or her customary environment. Due to the words "functional evaluation" and the awareness of speech-language, occupational therapy, and physical therapy evaluations, some have interpreted that the only way to request assistance is through a formal event called an "assistive technology evaluation."

The law, however, does not specify or define the term *assistive technology evaluation*. There is no stipulation stating that an evaluation needs to be a formal process resulting in a report. Rather, the act of evaluating can (and perhaps should) be informal. There is also no stipulation that the act of evaluating needs to be completed by one individual; the act of evaluating can be a collaborative, multidisciplinary, and/or interdisciplinary effort.

If the term *functional evaluation* in the law is interpreted to mean "evaluating to help determine needs," then school districts can offer flexible models for how to help IEP teams determine necessary technologies. This allows IEP teams to take advantage of these different structures based on the circumstance, situation, and needs of the student. Just as there is no singular tool that will fit every student, there is likely no singular process that will fit every situation when evaluating needs. Offering an array of options for how to determine a student's needs (and being open to creating even more options) provides the greatest opportunity to meet the needs of every student. And whichever option the IEP team chooses can still be documented in the IEP.

There are a few reasons why IEP teams might choose to formalize a request for assistance by writing it into the IEP. Documenting the request serves to protect all the parties involved; it provides verification that the IEP team has met its obligations, offering assurance to the family that the appropriate and necessary actions have been performed. Furthermore, when a request is documented in the IEP, future educators working with the student can read exactly what has happened in the past. Although documentation can also occur outside the IEP, documenting as much as possible in the IEP keeps everything in one location for current and future teams to review. Finally, as hard as people may work to build relationships and gain each other's trust, sometimes it just doesn't work out that way. If anyone ever feels uncomfortable, unsettled, or unsure, it is appropriate to put everyone's minds at ease by documenting the request for assistance in the IEP. Fulfilling the obligations written in the request will go a long way toward building that trust.

ASSESSING RATHER THAN EVALUATING

One of the best resources for helping people design and develop programs related to ensuring the proper consideration of technology is *Assessing Students' Needs for Assistive Technology: A Resource Manual for School District Teams*, 5th edition (2009) (bit.ly/asnatchapters) from the Wisconsin Assistive Technology Initiative (wati.org). As the authors note, the words *evaluation* and *assessment* hold different meanings in education. An evaluation is often perceived as a one-time action performed by a professional or expert in the discipline. Although evaluations might produce recommendations or offer suggestions for new tools and strategies, their primary function is to determine a student's eligibility to qualify as a person with a disability. Assessments, by contrast, are ongoing actions conducted by relevant stakeholders. Assessing what a student needs in order to achieve his or her goals does not impact a student's eligibility status, and evaluating if a student is eligible to receive special-education services has no bearing on assessing which tools and strategies a student might need to achieve goals.

How to Document a Request for Assistance in the IEP

When documenting a request for assistance, the IEP team specifies the details of what is expected to occur. The team should avoid using vague terms like *assessment, evaluation,* and/or *consultation* unless they are explicitly defined in a location accessible to all members of the IEP team, as these terms can be interpreted differently by different people. And even with specific definitions, using one word to describe the act of assisting in the determination of options can still lead to incorrect interpretations. Instead, write an entire statement describing the specific actions the IEP team wants to happen. The more explicitly the statement is written, the better the chances that everyone will have the same expectations. The statement should include the following parameters whenever requesting assistance in the IEP:

1. What is the problem?

    - What, exactly, does the IEP team need help determining?

    - What goal is the student having trouble accomplishing?

2. Who is going to assist the IEP team?

    - Will it be someone knowledgeable in the area in which the problem is occurring?

    - Should it be a related-service staff member?

    - Might it be appropriate for more than one staff member to provide the assistance?

3. What specific actions should be taken by the professional(s) helping to determine options for support?

    - Should the professional(s) providing assistance review relevant documentation pertaining to the student, and if so, which documents should be reviewed?

    - Should an observation in the child's customary environment occur during the time when the student is working on the specified goal?

    - Do interviews with the educators, the parents, and/or the student need to be conducted?

4. How is the assistance going to be documented?

    - Will a list of options be generated and provided for the IEP team to consider?

5. By when will the specific actions occur?

   - What is a reasonable amount of time in which to complete the actions being requested?

   - By when will the IEP reconvene to review the actions taken?

Sample Requests for Assistance in an IEP

The IEP team might write something similar to one of these three examples:

1. The case manager will meet with an accessible-design facilitator, speech-language pathologist, occupational therapist, reading specialist, and/or any other staff member(s) with knowledge relevant to reading difficulties to review progress notes, assessment data, and the current IEP, which includes the goal(s) pertaining to reading and provides a list of potential options for intervention within 60 business days. The IEP team will reconvene within 10 business days of having the list of options presented.

2. Within 30 business days, an accessible-design facilitator, speech-language pathologist, and/or any other staff member(s) with knowledge relevant to communication difficulties will review the IEP along with goal(s) pertaining to communication, observing the student in his customary educational environment, interviewing stakeholders (including the student), and providing a list of potential options for intervention within 65 business days. The IEP team will reconvene within 10 business days of having the list of options presented.

3. Within 30 business days, an accessible-design facilitator will meet with the case manager to review the IEP and coach the case manager through a process for considering needs related to technology selection, acquisition, and implementation. The IEP team will reconvene within 10 business days of the coaching session to use the process to consider and determine the technology necessary to ensure the student continues to have access to a free appropriate public education.

LEADING WITH TRUST

Imagine a parent contacting an educational experience designer to brainstorm ideas. During that conversation, the EED states that she will meet with the accessible-design facilitator to brainstorm some more, and following that meeting, a list of ideas will be provided to the parent.

A short time later, the EED and accessible-design facilitator meet (possibly even inviting the parent to take part in the meeting), discuss the student, generate a list of ideas, and then send that on to the parent, explaining that they'll be implementing some of the options.

In this scenario, everyone has done exactly what they promised to do. When every person does this, trust grows. Goodwill wins, relationships grow stronger, and confidence is emboldened—all to the benefit of the student and his or her right to a free appropriate public education.

Whenever possible, lead with trust.

The Hidden Costs of Requesting Assistance

Requesting assistance to consider technology has associated costs. For instance, time is a limited commodity, so asking someone to provide assistance has a double cost. The age-old adage remains true: time is money. No matter the job title, those providing assistance will expect to be compensated for their time; and this compensation has fiduciary consequences that impact budgets, taxes, and livelihoods.

The cost of asking for and receiving someone's help can be calculated (if anyone is so inclined) to determine an average dollar amount per request. This calculation can be used as a metric for making staffing decisions, altering policies and practices, and generally informing administrators and the public about where and how monies are being spent. To make the calculation, one would need the following variables:

> If **a** is the average time it takes to request and receive assistance, **b** is the average hourly rate of the person making the request, **c** is the average time it takes for the person being asked to provide this assistance, and **d** is the

average hourly rate of the person assisting in the request, then **e** is the average hourly cost of making and assisting with the request:

$$(a \times b) + (c \times d) = e.$$

Note: This calculation only accounts for the time it takes to request, provide, and review the provision of assistance. The time it takes to acquire a support (tool) and train individuals on how to use this support would have an additional cost per hour.

The number of hours in the day are finite, and the expense associated with choosing to take one action over another does not have a formula associated with calculating the cost; the cost is related to the opportunity. When staff are engaged in the task of providing assistance for an individual, they are not necessarily working on other projects that might benefit the masses (such as creating a professional-development opportunity).

When determining which action to take, ask which action will make the most significant impact in the shortest amount of time. What gives you the biggest bang for your buck? Building professional-development experiences, creating support mechanisms, and serving on collaborative committees where decisions are made for the entire educational agency are all examples of opportunities that also cost time. With limited time and resources, which opportunity are you going to choose?

AWESOME INSIGHT

Time is a limited resource—use it wisely. Collect media and other artifacts during daily activities so they can be used in longer-term initiatives or projects that impact the entire agency, like building an online course, creating instructional videos, making an informative website, or constructing any other professional-development experiences.

Costs related to time and opportunity can be perceived as invisible by those not consciously thinking of them when working for or with an education agency. As such, requesting assistance can seem like an entitlement or a free resource. Conversations about the costs in time and opportunity shape perspectives and bring about a greater understanding of the bigger picture. Dollars—often tax dollars—are being used to pay for the time being spent, and there is a responsibility that comes with spending that money. Being transparent about how those dollars are spent reminds people about the true cost associated with the decisions being made.

Synergistic Value

Costs in money, time, and opportunity should not be used as a reason to not ask for help. The actions taken to help others have the potential to effectively alter a student's future life permanently and for the better. The options provided, along with the decisions surrounding the implementation of these options, have social, emotional, educational, and financial ramifications that impact a student's entire life. Often, this assistance is what can turn a situation around—not just for the student but for everyone working with that student. If you change the life of even one student, isn't it worth it?

The ripple effect of providing assistance can be of significant and immeasurable value. Providing options to an educator helps them shape educational experiences for every student with whom they work, now and in the future. And if you change the impact of even one educator, isn't it also worth it?

CHAPTER 8

Providing Assistance

Assistance has been requested! Help is needed! You've been given the task of helping an educational experience designer (or an IEP team) who is considering technology for a student. What do you do? How do you do it? When are you providing assistance? What does it all look like?

In this chapter, you'll:

1. Learn a process for providing assistance to those who determine what technology is necessary to ensure a free appropriate public education for all students.

2. Explore strategies for collecting evidence to support suggestions provided to those requesting assistance.

ISTE STANDARDS ADDRESSED

ISTE Standards for Educators 2a. Shape, advance, and accelerate a shared vision for empowered learning with technology by engaging with education stakeholders.

ISTE Standards for Educators 2c. Model for colleagues the identification, exploration, evaluation, curation, and adoption of new digital resources and tools for learning.

ISTE Standards for Educators 4d. Demonstrate cultural competency when communicating with students, parents, and colleagues and interact with them as co-collaborators in student learning.

ISTE Standards for Educators 6d. Model and nurture creativity and creative expression to communicate ideas, knowledge, and/or connections.

How to Provide Assistance: It's a RIOT!

When providing assistance, there is a series of actions that can help determine options. These actions are used to add information to each of the four areas of the SETT Framework and can be grouped into four functions: (R) reviewing documentation, (I) interviewing stakeholders, (O) observing the student, and (T) trying things out (see Table 8.1). Providing assistance is fun—so much fun that it is a RIOT! (*Note:* not every step is required with every assistance request. At times, only a review of the documentation or an interview with relevant educators is necessary to provide options.)

Table 8.1 RIOT Functions to Determine Assistance Options

Action	What or Who Is Involved
R – Review	• Most recent IEP • Evaluative reports • Progress notes and report cards • Communication logs • Student schedule • Student work samples
I – Interview	• Educators working with the student • Student's caregivers • Student (if applicable)
O – Observe	• Student working on the area or areas in need of support • Student in the customary educational environments
T – Try	• Introducing a new support to the student, inviting the student to try it out, and collecting evidence to determine potential usefulness/effectiveness

R—Review Documentation

Review the most recent documentation pertaining to the student. This documentation includes the most recent IEP, school-provided and disclosed external evaluative reports, progress notes, and report cards. Student work samples and his or her daily schedule might also be reviewed. Beyond specifying current performance and abilities, information from these documents adds insights into the efficacy of the tools and strategies that have previously been implemented with the student.

I—Interview Stakeholders

When providing assistance, conversations should take place with those who work with the student. At times, this might be the case manager, the educational experience designer, related service staff, administrators, the student himself, a family member, or any combination of these individuals. These conversations are crucial for gathering information, setting expectations for how assistance will be provided, and guiding the team through the decision-making process.

When interviewing each stakeholder, explore elements like a detailed review of the student's schedule, possibly starting from waking up in the morning until going to bed at night; discuss what the student enjoys most about the school experience and what the student would avoid or change about the school experience, if given a choice; draft a statement about which supports are working in the given situation or goal; and elicit a vision from the individual who might help implement a positive change to whatever problem led to the request for help in the first place. These conversations are of particular importance when interviewing the student. The student is the person who has the final say as to what will be used. By the end of the conversation, the person or persons providing the assistance, along with the person or persons providing the information, should have ideas for options that could bring about a change to the situation.

Good Questions to Ask

Providing assistance is more about helping others to understand their options and learn how to make their own least restrictive decisions than it is about providing them with solutions. One effective technique is to ask numerous questions relevant to the situation. Asking the right questions invites people to think about answers and the reasons why certain constructs exist. Providing assistance in this manner leads people to come to their own conclusions rather than imposing conclusions upon them. (People are more likely to embrace change when the idea for that change comes from within.)

Some good questions and evocative statements might include:

- Do you mind if we discuss the supports in your classroom?

- What would you like to see happen with this student that is different than what is currently happening?

- What do you envision the student accomplishing before the end of the year?

- What barriers do you see that are preventing the achievement of that goal?

- What will be necessary to remove those barriers?

- What do you think about the tasks the student is being asked to do? Given the option, would you or others choose to participate in these tasks?

- What are some ways the task could be redesigned to empower the student to take responsibility for his or her learning?

- What are some features of tools that might help the student take ownership of his or her learning?

- Suppose nothing changes. What's the worst thing that can happen? What does that mean for you? What does that mean for the student?

- What are some tools, strategies, and techniques that have been working well for the student? What types of lessons does the student get really jazzed about? On the flip side, what hasn't worked so well?

These questions and statements are just a few examples of what could be said to help people make their own decisions regarding what changes should be put in place to assist a student. They are intended to kick off a nonthreatening, disarming, thought-provoking, reflective conversation that leads people to form their own conclusions.

Now that you've read these questions, how could you see yourself using them to facilitate a discussion? What challenges do you see in learning to use them? For those who practice asking these types of questions and making these types of statements, the discussion becomes second nature. What steps might be necessary for you to learn to ask these types of questions?

Motivational Interviewing

One technique used by therapists when working with people who are making a big change in their lives, such as quitting smoking, losing weight, or giving up alcohol, is called "motivational interviewing." Motivational interviewing involves asking questions and using statements that bring about an intrinsic motivation to make a change rather than attempting to impose a change upon a person. The technique is useful for anyone working with educators in any consultative, facilitative, or coaching capacity, such as an accessible-design facilitator.

Learning the technique takes time and practice to execute effectively, but you are in luck: entire books, conferences, and communities of practice exist around it. If learning more about motivational interviewing is something you are interested in, what steps might you take to do so? (MINT: Motivational Interviewing Network of Trainers [motivationalinterviewing.org] is one resource to get you started.)

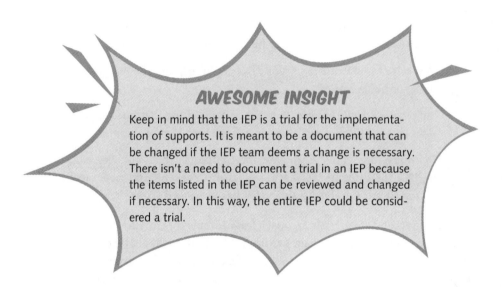

AWESOME INSIGHT

Keep in mind that the IEP is a trial for the implementation of supports. It is meant to be a document that can be changed if the IEP team deems a change is necessary. There isn't a need to document a trial in an IEP because the items listed in the IEP can be reviewed and changed if necessary. In this way, the entire IEP could be considered a trial.

O—Observe the Student

When called for, observe the student in the environment that relates to the tasks requiring assistance. If a student is demonstrating difficulty achieving math goals, then observe the student in a situation where math is the target of instruction. If the assistance request is related to accessing a computing device, then observe when the student is working with that device. Take notes about the student's performance and abilities while participating in these tasks, and use them to determine considerations for potential interventions, including changes in technology.

T—Try New Things

When working with a student, an opportunity might arise to allow the student to experiment with a tool or support that is new to them. This might involve inviting the student to experiment with an unfamiliar device, a feature of software he didn't know existed, a tool he is already familiar with that can be used in a different way, or adjustments to a task that could make it more accessible. The person providing assistance can gather initial impressions from the student and collect preliminary evidence regarding the experience. The following list contains sample questions to consider when trying a new support and generating relevant information on the area where support is needed:

- How well does the student target cells of a specific size on a communication device?

- What does the student think about using his voice to record his answers?

- By placing a switch in this position, can the student target and access it more consistently, compared to another position?

- Is this item too heavy to be carried around by the student?

- Should the pace of the text-to-speech voice be sped up or slowed down to suit the listener?

Trying new supports generates valuable feedback, including level of success in completing the task, degree of personal satisfaction from using the support, and any adjustments that could make the experience of using the support even better. The evidence collected while trying these things establishes a foundation upon which considerations for future changes or additions to technology can be made.

For example, during practice, an athlete might try a new piece of equipment or a new technique to see if it is a good fit. This might be a different type of glove, shoe, padding, or any gear that might add some benefit. Trying something for a few test plays, throws, pitches, hits, swings, and passes to see what the player thinks about the experience is a short form of assessment. Enough observable evidence can still be collected in this short time to determine if it is something the player might like to continue using, though the player can change her mind if a variable changes.

Trying something is very different than trialing something. Trialing an item is like conducting a scientific experiment, where there is an attempt to control variables. Defined and agreed-upon parameters are set regarding duration, evidence collection, personnel, and implementation techniques. Trialing a piece of sporting equipment involves multiple attempts in the use of that equipment—attempts to account for all the variables for the conditions of the trial. Trials take more effort and time to conduct when compared to trying.

In relation to the determination of educational supports, trying something takes place during the provision of assistance. Trying something provides information that can be used by members of the IEP team regarding implementation. Once something is implemented, a student will either continue to demonstrate difficulty achieving the goal or improve; and an IEP team can reconvene at any time to discuss and adjust the program. For this reason, the IEP team can confidently implement a support without a trial. If the data is showing the student isn't making progress toward achieving the goal, the supports can be adjusted. If the data is showing the student is making progress, well then, score!

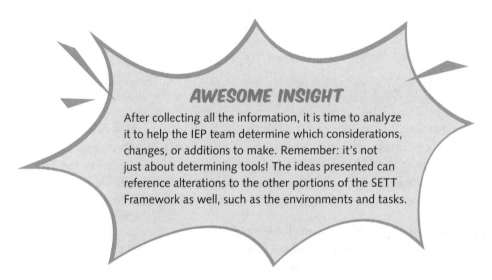

AWESOME INSIGHT

After collecting all the information, it is time to analyze it to help the IEP team determine which considerations, changes, or additions to make. Remember: it's not just about determining tools! The ideas presented can reference alterations to the other portions of the SETT Framework as well, such as the environments and tasks.

Multiple Tools and Means for Collecting Evidence

You can't effectively provide assistance without the proper tools for evidence collection. At a minimum, you need some way to collect notes, take pictures, record audio, and capture video. A tablet of some sort typically offers these functions and gives a person the ability to keep the data organized.

Note-taking applications such as Noteability, OneNote, SoundNote, and ATEval2Go (again, the author discloses he is the author of this application) are all options for evidence collection. Regardless of which one you use, it is important that the application saves data locally to the device or to a cloud-based server sanctioned by the school district. Laws such as the Child's Online Privacy Protection Rule (15 US Code § 6501), which is specific to children under the age of 13; the Family Educational Rights and Privacy Act (20 USC § 1232g; 34 CFR Part 99); and the Individuals with Disabilities Education Improvement Act (PL 108-446) provide guidance pertaining to acceptable and unacceptable sharing of identifiable data, including names and images. These regulations stipulate that personal and confidential data about a student should not be stored on servers accessible by people who don't have permission to access that data. Always be sure your note-taking application complies with your school district's policy on data collection and management.

Also important: remember to take pictures of everything! Take pictures of the instructional supports used, like the visuals on the walls, mounted to tables and desks, and hanging around people's necks. Take pictures of the student engaging in tasks that demonstrate his or her abilities. Pictures might include screenshots of what was accessed or produced on a device, or snapshots of paper-based work samples. Then, once you've taken all the pictures you can, take some more! The objective is to include enough images in the documentation of provision of assistance to complete the picture of the current environments, tasks, and supports.

Like images, videos can also be collected to represent the educational experience of the student. Videos of the student engaging in tasks or trying out a new piece of equipment, if collected, can be included in the documentation of provision of assistance. Images and videos provide observable and irrefutable evidence of what occurred, helping IEP team members come to conclusions about what should or should not be implemented.

Most schools have a media release form signed by parents or guardians that allows for the use of photographs. Be sure you have proper permission to use the student's image in this documentation of provision of assistance. Not having permission might mean only including images that don't contain identifying characteristics. This might include pictures of supports, hands, and/or other perspectives from which a student's face is obscured, as from behind or over the shoulder. Alternatively, if permission is not granted, the portion of an image containing a student's face could be pixelated or blocked out using an image-manipulation application.

CHAPTER 9

Documenting Assistance

Video gamers have a saying: "Screenshot or it didn't happen." You might imagine how some gamers might brag to online friends about unearthly accomplishments, feats, and exploits. To keep the giant fish tales under control, gamers imposed this simple rule. You either provide some evidence—specifically in the form of a screenshot or video—or you can save the fantastical story to regale a noob who doesn't know any better.

If you've provided any form of assistance, then your next step is to prove it. You've likely planted some seeds that you hope will blossom into beautiful flowers through dialogue and guiding questions. Now, it's time to document your work.

In this chapter, you'll:

1. Explore how to document assistance once it has been provided.

2. Examine samples of documentation of assistance provided.

ISTE STANDARDS ADDRESSED

ISTE Standards for Educators 2a. Shape, advance, and accelerate a shared vision for empowered learning with technology by engaging with education stakeholders.

ISTE Standards for Educators 2b. Advocate for equitable access to educational technology, digital content, and learning opportunities to meet the diverse needs of all students.

ISTE Standards for Educators 2c. Model for colleagues the identification, exploration, evaluation, curation, and adoption of new digital resources and tools for learning.

ISTE Standards for Educators 3b. Establish a learning culture that promotes curiosity and critical examination of online resources and fosters digital literacy and media fluency.

ISTE Standards for Educators 4d. Demonstrate cultural competency when communicating with students, parents, and colleagues and interact with them as cocollaborators in student learning.

ISTE Standards for Educators 5c. Explore and apply instructional design principles to create innovative digital learning environments that engage and support learning.

ISTE Standards for Educators 7c. Use assessment data to guide progress; and communicate with students, parents, and education stakeholders to build student self-direction.

How to Document that Assistance Was Provided

Documentation should occur whether or not assistance was requested in the IEP. Providing, maintaining, and referring to the documentation proves the act of assisting took place while simultaneously providing a digital trail to which others can refer. This documentation can then be used to help make future decisions.

Documentation tells the story of what has been attempted, what has been implemented, and what progress has been made. Documentation also offers the talking points necessary for the IEP team to decide which of the options might be necessary to ensure a free appropriate public education.

Length and detail of documentation may vary upon circumstances. For example, the documentation could include the following elements:

- A restatement or summary of the problem to explain why the assistance was asked for in the first place

- A list of previously attempted and current interventions, along with descriptions of effectiveness

- A description of the observed evidence (cold, hard facts, not opinions or impressions), including facts about the student, environments, and tasks as witnessed during an observation or as stated by the educators interviewed

- Options for the team to consider that might help with the stated problem

- Resources in the form of links to research articles, tutorials, and additional media that supports the options provided

Once drafted, it's time to share the documentation of assistance with the case manager, who, in turn, can share it with the entire IEP team.

BE LIKE BRUCE AND BARRY

Bruce Wayne—you probably know him better by his superhero name: Batman. Although it's not typically highlighted in the Batman movies, in the comics, Bruce Wayne is known for his detective skills.

When you are in the stages of collecting information, embrace your inner Bruce Wayne. Collect data in the form of facts, leaving no stone unturned. And whenever you're in doubt, transform into Batman, enlisting your superhuman-like efforts. (Don't hang anyone over the edge of a building to get information, though!) When collecting evidence, be the human and the superhero combined: the world's greatest detective.

After all the facts have been gathered, it is time to hang up the cape and change the color of the cowl. It's time to embrace your inner Barry Allen—the secret identity of The Flash—whose day job is that of a forensic scientist who analyzes crime

scenes. Like Barry, be methodical and thorough as you complete the documentation of the assistance provided; but once you're done, switch to The Flash, sending
the documentation as quickly as possible. Don't let multiple instances of providing
assistance stack up. Take them in the order that they come, then work
to get the information out to people as soon as possible.

Expeditious documentation benefits you, the educators, and the student. The
sooner the IEP team has the information, the sooner they can do something with
it. And the sooner you've provided the documentation, the sooner it is off your
perpetually filling plate. Schedules should be arranged so time is allocated appropriately. For example, if a visit is scheduled for a Monday morning, consider blocking
off Monday afternoon or Tuesday morning to complete the documentation of
assistance. Then, when reporting the evidence, be the fastest person alive.

Multiple Means of Documentation

Documenting the provision of assistance in determining options to support a
student should be provided in multiple formats. At times, depending on the extent
of the assistance and what's been requested, the situation may call for brevity or for
something more extensive and multimodal. A quick, text-only summary via email
might be all that is necessary to outline a few options. At other times, multiple
media types and sources might be required to adequately and effectively describe
the situation.

Documentation could include text, images (such as pictures, drawings, charts, and
infographics), videos (including animations), and audio samples. Documentation
could be presented in a variety of file formats as well, including ePub or PDF. The
more modalities provided, the more accessible and understandable the information
becomes. If content for student learning is available in a variety of formats, then so,
too, should be the documentation of provision of assistance.

Report Retort

The noun *documentation* does not necessarily need to equate to the term *report*.
As a student grows, makes progress, and acquires new skills, it is necessary to keep
considering which tools and strategies are necessary to ensure continued success.

If learning does not stop, the evaluation of what might be necessary to keep that learning happening should not stop either.

Unintentionally, the drafting of an official-looking report can sometimes lead people to believe that the act of providing assistance has ended when, in fact, the report is just one part of the ongoing process of determining what a student needs. Documentation should occur, but there isn't any specification in any laws for what that needs to look like. Although the report can be formally presented, it need not be a document with official letterhead that takes hours to write. Unless specified by the IEP team that this is necessary for some reason, documentation can be provided in whatever manner is least restrictive to convey the information. Documentation could be (and is most frequently) an email summary.

AWESOME INSIGHT

Imagine providing a link to an audio or video file stored on a secured server (just like where the text of an email is stored) containing a description and considerations from the person or persons providing the service. Accessibility of the documentation of assistance provided should also be considered. Ideally, the documentation would be provided in multiple ways (just like providing content to students). At the very least, the documentation should be presented to the IEP team digitally so those who require technology to experience it can do so.

Support from the Experiences of Others

IEP team members might appreciate supports shared by other professionals, parents, or students out in the wider world who have experience using similar tools and strategies. Sharing the experiences of individuals who have already worked through similar experiences helps paint the picture of what might be possible. (Creating a visualization of one potential future brings it one step closer to reality, inspiring questions like "One day my student could be like that person. ... How do we get there?) When providing documentation, links to resources sharing the experiences of others is a powerful way to shape expectations. Examples of resources like this might include links to the following:

- Blog posts

- Podcast episodes

- Video testimonials

- Social-media support sites

Facts versus Opinions

When you roll a die, you get a result—this is a fact. Cards have two sides—a back and a front; this is another fact. Someone won the game? Fact, fact, facitty-fact! "It seemed like everyone enjoyed playing." That is *not* a fact; that is an opinion. "This game is fun." Again, that's an opinion. "This is the best game ever!" Yup, yet another opinion.

Facts are binary—they either happened or they didn't. There is no gray area or subjectivity within them. Facts are black or white—they are not any shade of gray. Opinions are impressions based on facts. Opinions are formed from the facts.

When it comes to educational reporting of any type, it is important to keep the facts and the opinions in their proper places and not intermix them. Meshing them together adds confusion. At times, making decisions about which supports are necessary can be difficult. By clearly delineating between what is fact and what is opinion by keeping the two separated, isolated, and contained to their proper areas, the consumer can make informed decisions about which supports to implement.

When restating the problem as described by the IEP team, reiterate the problem as a fact, which cannot be refuted. Start the sentence using language such as:

- "The request for assistance stated [insert statement]."

- "A member of the IEP team approached the accessible-design facilitator and inquired about supports to assist the student in achieving [insert goal]."

Similarly, when documenting supports previously attempted or currently in place, stick to the facts. Examples might include:

- "Visual supports are on the student's desk."

- "The student has access to the LAMP (Language Acquisition through Motor Planning) Words for Life (WFL) application on a personally owned iPad."

- "The parents report that the student attends private speech therapy twice a week after school."

When listing these supports, a statement regarding any data or evidence pertaining to the effectiveness of the support should also be applied. These, too, should be written as a statement of fact:

- "The teacher reports that the student does not appear to use or reference the visuals on the desk."

- "According to the most recent progress notes, the student has used over 25 different words spontaneously (without prompting) using the LAMP Words for Life application over the last year."

- "The parents report that despite both public and private speech therapy, they feel that not enough progress is being made."

When reporting upon what was witnessed during an observation, again, stick to the facts:

- "The student was presented with …"

- "The student completed 9 out of 10 …"

- "The student used the following words …"

- "The student wrote the following sentences …"

- "The educator working with the student stated …"

Opinions do not belong in the same area as observed evidence. The only area where opinions are warranted is in the presentation of the considerations that might address the problem. This is where deductive analysis of the presented facts mixes with experience to help educators and other IEP team members develop informed impressions of what might assist the situation. Then the IEP team uses these considerations to make their own informed decisions about what alterations might be necessary to assist the student.

Statements of opinions might start with phrases like:

- "Consider the implementation of …"

- "According to the statements made by multiple IEP team members, it appears that …"

- "The evidence collected up to this date appears to indicate that the following supports and changes might be effective …"

Considerations or Options, Not Recommendations or Suggestions

In many team sports, one of the critical actions to winning is passing. In hockey, you pass the puck. In soccer and basketball, you pass the ball. Heck, even in made-up games like Harry Potter's quidditch, you pass the quaffle! When someone is in the right position to pass, makes the decision to pass, and executes that pass so perfectly another player scores because of it, it is a called an "assist." Statistics are kept on how many assists each player has per game.

These statistics show the coaches how effective each player is without relying on scoring as the only metric. If scoring were the only metric used to evaluate player performance, there would likely be a lot more people trying to score on their own and a lot fewer helping teammates score. Likewise, whoever provides assistance to an IEP team has the role of providing assists, not scoring. Their role is to set up the IEP team with what they need to score.

Undoubtedly, when going through the process of providing assistance, the person doing so will have ideas on how to improve the given situation. The entire point of the exercise is to generate ideas that might help the IEP team consider needs. Any and every time someone attempts to provide assistance, that person will generate ideas on how to help the student.

A word of caution: When documenting these ideas, it might be tempting to present them as recommendations. The word *recommendation*, however, is often related in people's minds to *expert advice*. When an expert gives a recommendation, it forces people into the position of either listening to that expert or going against that expert. Likewise, when a recommendation is given, it forces the IEP team to choose between agreeing or disagreeing with it. At times, there might be some IEP team members who agree with the recommendations and others who don't. This works against the idea that members should work together to make common decisions.

Remember, the role of the person providing assistance is to empower the IEP team to make their own decisions. To that end, this person should document her or his ideas by laying out options and/or considerations but not recommendations and/or suggestions. Fortunately, there are a variety of strategies that facilitate and reinforce this goal of empowering the IEP team as the force making a decision, including the following:

- Titling the section of documentation "Ideas to Consider" or "Considerations"

- Including a sentence or two specifying how it is the IEP team's responsibility to make decisions, which also guides them to consider least restrictive options

- Beginning each description of an option with a phrase similar to "Consider inviting the student to [insert support you are inviting the student to use]" or "Consider the student's need for [insert support that might be implemented to guarantee a free appropriate public education]"

- Separating two or more similar considerations with the word "or," giving the IEP team the ability to choose between them

- Listing the pros and cons of two or more potential supports to draw a comparison among their different features

Documenting options for consideration using any combination of these strategies helps facilitate the idea that it is the members of the IEP team who make decisions about what should be implemented and not those providing assistance.

Optional Features for Documentation

When creating documentation of the assistance provided, consider the benefits of including the following elements.

A Statement of Reconvening

Provide a standard and consistent statement reminding anyone reviewing the documentation that it is the IEP team's responsibility to decide upon the necessity and inclusion of any consideration in the IEP. Here is a sample statement:

> *It is the responsibility of the case manager to share this documentation with the entire IEP team. It is the responsibility of the IEP team to discuss the necessity and implementation of the considerations.*

Bonus Considerations

Sometimes, an IEP team doesn't know what it doesn't know. Despite attempting to keep the considerations focused on the areas of concern listed by the IEP team, at times, those providing assistance might have additional ideas that might help the educators and/or the students. In these instances, another section that could be added when documenting the provision of assistance is "Bonus Considerations." A statement could be added that explicitly calls attention to the fact that these considerations are not related to the areas for which assistance was requested. A sample statement:

> *This documentation offers considerations to support the IEP team in making decisions pertaining to the specific areas for which assistance was requested. Additionally, the IEP team might wish to consider the following options, ideas, tools, strategies, or supports.*

A Statement of Everlasting Assistance

Time marches on. Once the assistance has been provided and documented, the IEP team has met to discuss the considerations, and the considerations have been implemented, the story of the student continues. The next day comes, then the next year, and the student continues to have educational experiences. New opportunities for growth and learning are always on the horizon, and with them comes the potential for additional challenges.

A statement could be added to the documentation to remind the IEP team that the consideration of supports is an ongoing, fluid process during which any member of the IEP team can reach out to obtain further assistance. For example:

> *Consideration of supports is an ongoing process. Any member of the IEP team can request assistance for additional support at any time to discuss the educational needs of the student. Assistance can be requested by contacting the case manager.*

A Statement About the Least Restrictive Option

It is very likely that most of the members of the IEP team have never heard of the principles of the least dangerous assumption. Although the members might be familiar with the concept of the least restrictive environment, these same members might not consider applying that principle to supports other than where the student receives services. Consider the inclusion of a statement educating people about the notion of making decisions based on what will restrict the student the least—the least restrictive option. For example, consider the following sample statement that could be included with the considerations:

> *It is the responsibility of the IEP team to provide supports that will restrict the student in the least possible way to ensure a free appropriate public education.*

Step-by-Step Protocols for Consideration

For some IEP teams, requesting assistance will be a rarity; so the school personnel working on the team might not know the protocols involved in the process. Consider providing a checklist or other guidance to help the IEP team complete the task of appropriately considering and documenting the options. A sample checklist might include:

- A statement about where to save and archive the documentation of assistance provided

- A reminder that every member of the IEP team should receive a copy of the documentation of assistance

- A reminder that it is the responsibility of the IEP team to meet and discuss the considerations

- A reminder that IEP team decisions regarding the tools and strategies deemed necessary to ensure a free appropriate public education should be listed as accommodations

- A reminder to document in the IEP that accommodations requiring the acquisition of materials will be implemented in a timely manner

- A reminder to notify the provider(s) of assistance regarding any further actions necessary on his or her part

Wording of Suggested Accommodation(s)

The IEP team will be reviewing the options in the documentation of assistance provided and considering which, if any, should be included as accommodations within the IEP. To assist the IEP team in this endeavor, it is helpful to include potential wording for each option provided. This way, the IEP team doesn't need to struggle over how to word an accommodation from scratch.

Along with the accommodation wording, a statement on potential frequency and location could also be provided to clarify that the responsibility ultimately falls to the IEP team to make the final determination for the inclusion and wording of every accommodation. Remind people that the wording for the accommodation, frequency, and location are only suggestions and not predeterminations. A statement of this nature might be as follows:

> *These are potential wordings only. It is the responsibility of the IEP team to determine the accommodations/modifications necessary to ensure a free appropriate public education.*

A Statement About Media Usage

Educational agencies have different media usage policies. Ensure permission has been granted by the student's parents following the procedures outlined by the educational agency's media-release policies before including media in the documentation of assistance that might identify the student. Media that does not identify the student can (and should) still be included. A statement about how the media release or usage has been reviewed for this student could be included in the documentation.

For example:

All media other than text in this documentation is used in accordance with the educational agency's media-release policy.

Sample Documentation of Assistance Provided

Kevin just moved to his new high school. He has a younger brother who is new to the local middle school as well. Everything is new to Kevin, including his bedroom, his house, his neighborhood, his bus ride, and his entire school. Every person he meets is a new face. Kevin also has autism and has never produced a word verbally.

Kevin has access to a personally owned iPad with the TouchChat HD augmentative/alternative communication (AAC) application on it. When he arrived at his new school, his IEP stated that his primary form of communication is through gestures but that he is learning to use a communication device to indicate his wants and needs.

Within his first few days, the new educators working with Kevin discover that their data is not matching the perception they had after reading the IEP. Kevin primarily presses the same three words out of context. These words are the name of his dog, his uncle, and his father, who is often away on business. Use of his high-tech communication device is new to every educator working with him, including the speech-language pathologist.

The IEP team requested assistance from a speech-language pathologist familiar with using high-tech AAC devices, and it contacted an accessible-design facilitator to help Kevin meet his IEP goals related to communication. What follows is a documentation sample of how assistance was provided once requested by the IEP team.

Summary of Student Abilities

Kevin is a high school student who is new to the school. According to his most recent IEP, Kevin's primary form of expression is gestures, but he is attempting to learn how to use a communication device. He currently has access to a personal iPad with the TouchChat HD application. Kevin primarily presses specific cells on the device, such as the name of his dog and his father, but the staff has been unable to determine if these are being used for any communicative purpose. When Kevin does press these cells, the staff responds by modeling "not here" on the device. The IEP also states that Kevin follows one-step verbal directions paired with gestures or visuals.

What Does the IEP Team Need Help With?

Assistance was requested specifically to assist the current IEP team in helping Kevin learn the following:

- Producing single words (or more) to request an object or an action, including a protest

- Producing single words (or more) to convey location of a person, place, or thing

- Producing single words (or more) to respond to questions

- Producing single words (or more) to label on object or an action

What Supports Are In Place?

According to an interview with the student's parents, Kevin has had access to a different communication system approximately every three years since he was in preschool. These communication systems included a focus on sign language, then picture exchange, then a static display voice-output device, then a dynamic display voice-output device from Tobii Dynavox, then an iPad with the communication application Proloquo2Go, and currently, an iPad with the TouchChat HD application.

The parents report that they sometimes have difficulty locating words using this application. The parents also report that they have attended training on the LAMP (Language Acquisition through Motor Planning) Words for Life application and are curious about the benefits of this approach. His parents report that none of the previously provided supports proved to be a functional or effective form of communication for Kevin. The parents fear there has been a lack of consistency and modeling on all of the systems provided. For this reason, they have purchased and provided a second iPad to be used by the communication partner working with Kevin.

Observation Summary

Kevin was observed in a resource setting. At the beginning of the observation, Kevin was seated at a table with the instructional assistant working on the class activity of planting seeds. Kevin had an iPad with the TouchChat HD application. A second iPad was placed on a stand on the table as well, which also had the Touch-Chat HD application. Customizations had been made to the vocabulary set within both devices, including the addition of pictures of family members and Kevin's dog. During this activity, the observer began using an iPad to model words and phrases describing actions, like "I can do it"; "You do it"; "My turn"; "I want it, please"; "I want more, please"; "That"; "Please"; "You do it, please"; and other similar utterances.

Approximately 5 to 10 seconds of wait time was provided to give Kevin an opportunity to make a response before the communication partner initiated another utterance using the device. A least-to-most prompting method was used. At first, Kevin only pressed cells when direct gestural prompts were provided (for example, pointing at the cell Kevin should touch). After approximately 10 consecutive repetitions in which gestural prompts were provided, Kevin pressed the word "more" without a prompt to request another seed. Kevin participated in the lesson for the remainder of the block, where similar models were provided.

Options for Consideration by the IEP Team

Consider the implementation of an approach to language acquisition and communication that involves the use of a portable augmentative-communication device outfitted with the following:

1. Synthesized auditory output with a male voice

2. Direct selection of vocabulary on a touchscreen with a digital display

3. A language system with access to a potential vocabulary set of thousands of words and an emphasis on core vocabulary, where the most frequently used words are practiced most prevalently and the least number of presses is required to express each word

4. Limited movement of icons as vocabulary grows to maintain learned motor-access patterns

5. Consistent access to the device at home and at school

6. Frequent communication partners modeling language usage by using the same system as Kevin when interacting with him (a technique referred to as "aided language stimulation or input")

Table 9.1 illustrates possible accommodations for Kevin and the frequency with which they should be implemented.

Table 9.1 Potential Ways to Document Accommodations in an IEP

Accommodation(s)/Modification(s)*	Frequency*
Access to a portable voice-output device with the following: • A synthesized male voice • Direct selection of vocabulary on a digital display • Access to a potential vocabulary set of thousands of words with an emphasis on core vocabulary and the least number of presses required to express each word	During activities that require communication
Adult communication partners model language using the same language system as Kevin	When communicating with adult communication partners

These are potential wordings only. It is the responsibility of the IEP team to determine the accommodation(s)/modification(s) necessary to ensure a free appropriate public education.

Tables 9.2 and 9.3 show pros and cons in relation to Kevin's use of two iPad applications. The IEP team may wish to consider these pros and cons when deciding which application to implement.

Table 9.2 TouchChat HD Considerations

Pros	Cons
The student and his parents have been using the system and have some familiarity. No change is required in the system.	The parents report difficulty searching for where vocabulary is located.
The app is already available on multiple devices. There has already been significant time and effort invested in the application.	Some words are accessed in multiple locations, making it potentially more difficult to remember (and teach) where to access each word.
	Many high-frequency words are not represented with a picture. It is unclear whether Kevin needs picture supports, but visual supports have proven to be effective to help teach vocabulary to others.

Source: touchchatapp.com/apps/touchchat-hd-aac

Table 9.3 LAMP Words for Life Considerations

Pros	Cons
It's searchable.	Student and family have no familiarity with the system, and implementation would mean starting with yet another new system.
Words are found in consistent and unique locations. Meaningful repetition of motor movements can be built upon to teach these locations. In time, Kevin could potentially use motor memory to access words more readily.	If the IEP team agrees to implement this application, there would be no immediate cost to the family; however, in the future, when the student is no longer enrolled at the school, the family might have to take on the financial burden of acquiring additional personal copies of the application.
All words are represented with text and a picture. It is unclear whether Kevin needs picture supports, but visual supports have proven to be effective to help teach vocabulary to others.	

Source: aacapps.com/lamp/about

Additional Resources

Table 9.4 offers a list of possible resources to include at the end of documentation for a case like Kevin's.

Table 9.4 Additional Resources for Inclusion in the Documentation

Topic	Resource
The Goal of AAC—Spontaneous Novel Utterance Generation (SNUG)	• "Augmentative and Alternative Communication Decisions," American Speech-Language-Hearing Association (bit.ly/ashasnug) • Episode #151, "SNUG & Presuming Competence with AAC," The Compendium Blog of the A.T.TIPSCAST (bit.ly/attipscastsnug)
Research on the Language Acquisition through Motor Planning Instructional Approach	• "Research Insights into LAMP," Georgia Tech Tools for Life (bit.ly/lampresearchpdf)
Core (Most Frequently Used) Vocabulary Resources	• "Language via AAC ALL DAY LONG" (Bugaj, 2017), a slideshow on implementing core vocabulary all day long (bit.ly/techsplashaac) • PrAACtical AAC article archive on core vocabulary (praacticalaac.org/tag/core-vocabulary) • "Core Word Starter Lesson Plans," Language Lab (aaclanguagelab.com/resources/CoreStarter)
Aided Language Stimulation (Modeling Language on the Device)	• "Aided Language Stimulation Explained," a YouTube video by the author (bit.ly/alsexplained) • "Pivotal Skills for AAC Intervention: Aided Language Input," PrAACtical AAC (bit.ly/aidedlanguageskills) • How I Do It: Implementing Aided Language Input with Alicia Garcia, PrAACtical AAC (bit.ly/aidedlanguageimplementation)

Considering the Assistance Provided

You did it! You finished your documentation and sent it off to the relevant educator—the educational experience designer (who might be the case manager), an administrator, or any other professional who requested the assistance. What happens now?

Regardless of whether the request was initiated by an educator or by an IEP team, the next steps are the same: The receiver of the documentation sends it to the other members of the IEP team, and the IEP team considers the options. If the IEP team decides that they need to reconvene to consider the options, they do so. If the request did not originate with the IEP team, the IEP team may consider whether it is necessary to reconvene. Then the IEP team considers the options and decides if any of those options are required to ensure a student a free appropriate public education.

Providers of Assistance Typically Do Not Attend IEP Meetings

It might seem logical that the person or persons providing assistance to the IEP team should attend the IEP meeting to review the documentation and explain the assistance that has been provided. Perhaps the providers might shed some light on the options provided for consideration. However, as a general rule, the provider of assistance should not attend IEP meetings.

The reason is simple: the temptation is too great to lean upon the provider of assistance to make decisions for the IEP team. Not being present at the IEP meeting when the options are discussed reinforces the idea that the responsibility of determining what is necessary to ensure a free appropriate public education falls to the IEP team members. Making the final decisions empowers them to take ownership of their decisions; capacity is built. IEP team members should be encouraged to contact those providing the assistance before and after the IEP meeting, to inform their decision-making process while leaving that responsibility solely with the IEP team.

The time spent preparing an educational experience designer prior to an IEP meeting makes her or him knowledgeable about inclusionary practices and puts that person in the driver's seat. When EEDs speak about accessible practices that include potential technology implementation, alterations to the environments, and changes to the tasks, the message is that the EEDs are the experts on this inclusion. Unless the accessible-design facilitator is practiced at redirecting and guiding conversations without making decisions, there is an inherent risk that the other members of the IEP team will see the accessible-design facilitator as the expert, which defeats the purpose of being a facilitator.

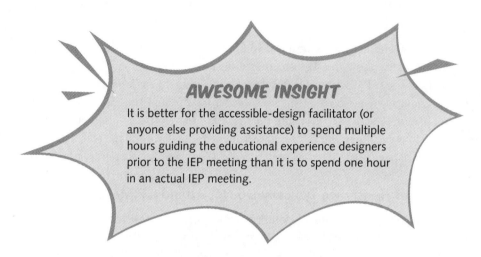

AWESOME INSIGHT

It is better for the accessible-design facilitator (or anyone else providing assistance) to spend multiple hours guiding the educational experience designers prior to the IEP meeting than it is to spend one hour in an actual IEP meeting.

"Not Now" Does Not Mean "Not Ever"

Your documentation of assistance outlines a series of options for consideration. For whatever reason, the case manager, student, or IEP team decided not to implement any of them. When this happens, it can feel frustrating or like you somehow failed in your duty as the provider of assistance.

However, what might feel like a failure in the present might just be a delayed success. A student might leave the present educational environment to transition to higher education or enter the workforce before realizing he or she would like to use a piece of technology. Imagine an individual going to someone in a university and saying, "This person at my old school once showed me how to do this cool thing on a computer, but I didn't use it. I think I want to use it now. Can you show me?"

Instances of delayed success make measuring impact and outcomes challenging. However, following student progress beyond the current educational environment is necessary to truly prove the outcomes made by providing assistance (see Figure 9.1).

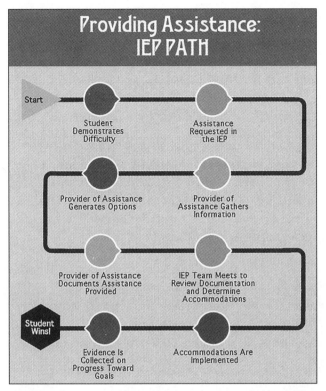

Figure 9.1 Steps to providing assistance when requested in an IEP.

Sample Service-Delivery Progress Report

There may be people who don't realize that support is being provided. A principal of a school who is in charge of day-to-day operations but not necessarily involved in every IEP meeting might not realize how much support is being provided by someone in the role of accessible-design facilitator. Collecting, documenting, and periodically reporting on the work being done keeps the effectiveness and essentialness of those coaching others in the forefront of everyone's mind—a critical consideration for agency leaders when it comes time to make budgetary decisions. Here is an example of a progress report that can be used to inform those of services rendered:

Dear [insert name of stakeholder],

It has been a pleasure serving as your accessible-design facilitator so far this year. I know we see each other sometimes in the building, but we don't always get a chance to talk about the work that's being done. To keep you informed about the services I've been delivering to your school, I wanted to provide you with some actual metrics. Think of it as a progress note for my direct services.

I should emphasize that this is only a brief synopsis and does not encompass all services provided. For instance, I worked on a committee to help bring about an on-demand course about dyslexia in the district's online learning portal. Any educator, including those at your school, can sign up to take it for free! That is just one example of a support not accounted for below. This report only pertains to the third quarter, between the dates of [insert dates].

Student Support

I've worked with educators to directly support 11 different students. This means I met with an educational experience designer, related service provider, other educator, and/or student to provide instructional support based on questions or concerns brought up by the case manager or IEP team.

Included in this support were approximately 14 instances of working with the educator or student to facilitate a discussion about available resources (some tool, strategy, technique, or other support). Some topics we looked at included augmentative communication, language development, creating and selecting accessible materials, and reading and writing supports.

Educator Support

Likewise, I've facilitated conversations with seven different educators that did not necessarily relate to any specific student. This means I've provided some sort of support based on questions or concerns generated by both special- and general educators to better support all students (which is awesome)!

Included in this support were approximately eight different instances of working with educators to help them discover or use available resources. Some topics we looked at included reading, writing, and math supports as well as augmentative-communication research and techniques.

Please let me know if you'd like any other details. It's been a pleasure working with the amazing staff at [insert name of school].

All the best,
[Your name], Accessible-Design Facilitator

Your Ticket to Ride

Ticket to Ride is a popular board game that invites players to compete for the ownership of railways that crisscross continental landmasses. Players draw cards, collect trains, and race each other to connect cities. As the game progresses, the board is filled with multicolored railway connections.

Like building connections on the game board, individuals working with different technologies build connections in their own brains regarding implementation and integration. Connecting two cities in Ticket to Ride is like connecting a student to necessary technology that they can use to meet an educational goal. To succeed in the game, a player needs trains; for the technology to succeed, those working with the technology might need to be trained.

Once the IEP team has decided what a student might require and documents those requirements in the IEP, the student, educators, and possibly, the family need to know how to effectively implement the technology. In many cases, depending on what is implemented, the educators will already know the features and functions of an item. In other cases, they will not. The accessible-design facilitator, or whoever provided the assistance, might conduct a training for the student, educators working with the students, and in some cases, the family of the students. Training and technical assistance is part of the federal definition of an assistive technology service. Chapter 12 of this book provides strategies pertaining to professional development and ongoing support through training.

Check schedules and set a destination. Get everyone a ticket and help them find their seats. When the training train leaves the station, it's time to think twice and do right by the team. All aboard!

CHAPTER **10**

Using Individual Needs to Design for the Masses

Educational experience designers are collecting evidence while working repeatedly with individuals, informing practices and technology that can be used to make decisions for the larger population of students. IEP teams are determining accommodations, either independently or with assistance. Those providing assistance (like accessible-design facilitators) are documenting options to help students with disabilities. Over time, trends emerge; and educators can analyze these trends to guide decisions about supports and practices as options for *every* student, not just those with an identified disability.

In this chapter, we'll:

1. Explore how technology needs for students with disabilities are applied to the larger population of students without disabilities.

2. Experience examples where technology was embraced by a larger population of students based on innovations applied for an individual with a disability.

ISTE STANDARDS ADDRESSED

ISTE Standards for Educators 2b. Advocate for equitable access to educational technology, digital content, and learning opportunities to meet the diverse needs of all students.

ISTE Standards for Educators 2c. Model for colleagues the identification, exploration, evaluation, curation, and adoption of new digital resources and tools for learning.

ISTE Standards for Educators 5a. Use technology to create, adapt, and personalize learning experiences that foster independent learning and accommodate learner differences and needs.

ISTE Standards for Educators 5c. Explore and apply instructional design principles to create innovative digital learning environments that engage and support learning.

ISTE Standards for Educators 7a. Provide alternative ways for students to demonstrate competency and reflect on their learning by using technology.

ISTE Standards for Educators 7c. Use assessment data to guide progress; and communicate with students, parents, and education stakeholders to build student self-direction.

Tier It Up

Multitiered system of supports (MTSS) is a framework for considering the needs of students encompassing the response-to-intervention (RTI) model, which breaks down supports into three distinct tiers—tier 1, tier 2, and tier 3—to classify and categorize levels of support provided to students. Tier 1 supports are research-based instructional practices provided to all students, including screenings and group interventions. Tier 2 supports are based on the targeted needs of students in small group settings. Tier 3 supports are provided solely to an individual after a comprehensive evaluation of that individual.

When describing technology supports, it might help to use this verbiage and terminology with people who are already familiar. The tiers in this model represent levels of intervention in addition to instruction, but they can be used to describe technological supports as well. When a tier 3 support is used by enough individuals, educators can consider strategies for making it available as a tier 2 or tier 1 support.

Assessing Features for the Larger Student Population

Remember way back in chapter 5 when we discussed how the function is more important than the specific tool and how a feature-matching process could be used to determine technology needs? Remember how we also mentioned attempting to select the least restrictive option for individual students?

When you use these techniques to select technology (or provide assistance to select technology), trends emerge. In time, you find that many students (with and without disabilities) tend to have similar needs. Educators can use these trends to put technology in place ubiquitously, for any student to access. The process for making these decisions for the masses is called "mass feature matching."

Mass Feature Matching: Data-Driven Decisions for the Masses

Educators can apply the technique of feature matching for individuals to the masses. One might think mass feature matching uses the same process as that of individual feature matching, but it is often difficult to anticipate all the current and future needs of the largest number of users. Alternatively (and possibly more accurately), the historical results of the individual feature matching process performed with or without assistance can be analyzed to make decisions about what should be applied universally.

For example, if, over the last five years, a school district has asked for assistance to be provided 100 times for students who have goals focused on improving writing, and 90 percent of the time, the individual feature matching process resulted in the acquisition and implementation of a tool that provided word prediction, educators could use that data to consider the acquisition of a word prediction tool ubiquitously. When the function is made universally accessible, it becomes less restrictive to implement. Providing a function via a tool that is immediately available as an option for anyone is a tier 1 support. When an educational experience designer is planning, she or he can count on that tool to be omnipresent to whomever needs it whenever it is needed. There is no time lost acquiring a tool because the tool is already in the environment.

The Best-Kept Secret in All of Education

There is a formula for choosing which features should be made available to every student as tier 1 supports: When documenting assistance, keep a running list of all the options in a separate spreadsheet or database. (A quick way to do this might be to add them to a survey tool, like a Google spreadsheet, in real time—at the moment of documentation [see Figure 10.1]. Here is an example: bit.ly/databaseofconsiderations.) You can use this cumulative data of considerations provided to determine frequency of use. Similarly, create a running list of all the accommodations used in every IEP. (Some online IEP systems have a data-export feature, which allows for the extraction of specific fields, such as accommodations.) Again, use this cumulative data to determine which accommodations are used most frequently. Combine and analyze these two data points to establish which features of technology are recommended, implemented, and deemed necessary most often. Then, if not already available as a tier 1 support, make these features available to every student, regardless of ability.

Consideration	Topic	Specific Name of Tool	Function of Tool
Record audio samples of student reading aloud. Student and/or a teacher document the length of time and number of errors. Periodic samples recorded and analyzed. Student charts progress (possibly earning badges and challenging himself to beat his previous goal, not unlike making progress in a video game). Compare audio samples from two different times to hear the improvements.	Reading/Literacy	Audacity, Voice Memos	Audio Recording
Measure readability of passages student is reading.	Reading/Literacy	Readability Feature of MS Word	Reading Measurement
Use the text to speech to listen to text and to edit his own written work.	Writing/Composition	Read&Write for Google Chrome	Text-To-Speech
Use a word-cloud generator to discover/investigate themes. Student places text from a passage into a word cloud generator to create a visualization of the words in the passage whereby the most frequently used words appear the largest. Themes become apparent based on the most frequently used words.	Reading/Literacy	Wordle.net	Word-Cloud Generation
Online or digital graphic organizers used to structure and organize content.	Reading/Literacy	Mindomo.com, Mindmeister.com, or Lucidchart.com	Graphic Organizer
Create something tangible by "touching" different parts of a story to remind the student of the different story elements. A story rope is one such strategy, but any tangible object could be used, such as Legos of different colors, to help draw the connections.	Reading/Literacy	Legos, Paper Images	Story Sequencing/Retelling
Line up numbers in mathematical problems.	Math	Modmath	Mathematical Computational Organizers

Figure 10.1 Sample database of considerations.

A Formula for Mass Implementation

Use a version of the following mathematical formula to do a cost–benefit comparison, and let the numbers speak for themselves. The formula relates specifically to instances when a provision of assistance had been requested (to obtain technology not already in the educational environment. Variations of this formula can be used when provision of assistance has not been requested and IEP teams have developed accommodations on their own. If exact numbers are not available, use estimated values. (You can use this template to make your own: bit.ly/massimplementationcalculationsheet.)

If **a** is the average time it takes to make the request for assistance, **b** is the average time it takes to conduct a document review of materials related to the request for assistance (analyze current IEP, evaluations, progress notes, etc.), **c** is the average time it takes to provide the assistance (travel, observation, interviews, etc.), **d** is the average time it takes to document assistance provided, **e** is the average time it takes to review and consider the documentation as an IEP team, and **f** is the average time it takes to acquire the tool that does the needed function documented in the IEP, then **g** is the total average time it takes to request, provide, and review assistance:

$$a + b + c + d + e + f = g;$$

and if **h** is the average time it takes to train all the educators at school on the function provided by the tool, **i** is the time it takes to train the family on this function, and **j** is the time it takes to train the student on this function, then **k** is the total average time it takes to provide training:

$$h + i + j = k;$$

and if the two average times are combined, then **l** is the total average time it takes to implement a function of a tool acquired for every individual who might require that feature:

$$g + k = l.$$

If **l** is multiplied by **m**, the number of individual students who have gone through this process per year, **n** is the total average time it takes (or the cost of process) to acquire a device not already in the environment:

$$l \times m = n.$$

Here is the formula for the total average cost of process (**n**) in its entirety:

$$[(a + b + c + d + e + f) + (h + i + j)] \times m = n.$$

Once calculated, repeat the formula, replacing time with money to determine the average financial cost to acquire a device not already in the environment per individual student. Once these numbers have been attained, they can be compared to the time and financial costs associated with the acquisition and maintenance of providing that feature to all students. Continuing to acquire a tool for specific individuals in the face of evidence that shows this is no longer efficient would be impractical. Instead, implement the function (and the tool that provides this function) in a way that makes it an immediately accessible option for any student to use as a tier 1 support.

Three Practical Examples

What follows are three separate examples based on actual events, which illustrate how accommodations led to features used by larger populations of students.

The Birth of the Flipped Classroom

Back in 2011, when Mr. Kale was a ninth-grade algebra teacher, he had a problem. He had been teaching algebra for years and felt very comfortable with how his class operated. Students came in, and he presented a lesson on the interactive whiteboard for the first 20 minutes (approximately) out of a 90-minute block. The students practiced the skill presented, and he walked around as they worked, giving suggestions to clarify and illustrate different aspects of the content. An educational assistant was present to help ensure that any students with disabilities were provided with the necessary accommodations. For Mr. Kale, this process worked smoothly. Then one day, he got a new student.

At the end of the previous school year, the IEP team (comprised of educators from the middle school and one representative from Mr. Kale's high school) wrote an accommodation stating that the student needed to have access to video recordings of classroom content in mathematics. (To ensure a free appropriate public education, the student needed the ability to rewatch video of the lessons.) The IEP team specified that supplemental videos of mathematical concepts would not be sufficient to help the student learn the content. The IEP team agreed that the student, when doing assignments and when studying, needed the ability to rewatch the same exact math lesson that had previously been presented.

When Mr. Kale read the accommodation, he was none too thrilled. He was an algebra teacher, not a videographer. He had no clue how to set up a video camera in his classroom in such a way that the student could see and hear everything that was being presented, let alone how to transfer that video to the student if he was successful in recording it.

A little worried, Mr. Kale reached out for help. He asked for a meeting with the instructional-technology resource teacher, Ms. Pickleson, who worked at the school, to brainstorm a workable solution. Ms. Pickleson suggested using the screen-recording function of the interactive whiteboard software to record videos of anything shown or done on the interactive whiteboard. Mr. Kale learned how to launch the screen-recorder function and save the resulting video file. He also learned how to pause the video recording when he or a student wasn't directly presenting on the interactive whiteboard. Once he had the video file, Mr. Kale opted to place the video on his website. He wasn't sure how to use the school's learning-management system, but he had previously been to a training on how to load content to the website allocated to him by the school.

With a little practice and a healthy dose of trial and error, Mr. Kale began creating videos of his class lessons and placing them on the web. The video files ranged anywhere from 10 to 30 minutes, depending on the content being delivered. The new student was shown how to access the files on Mr. Kale's website, and on occasion, Mr. Kale pointed other students to the content as well. When any student was absent, Mr. Kale suggested that the student go to his website during study hall and watch the lesson to get caught up. When struggling to complete an assignment, Mr. Kale invited students to rewatch the lesson. And before a summative assessment, Mr. Kale reminded his students about the videos, inviting them to rewatch content in areas where they needed more practice.

Ms. Pickleson, aware of the new strategy Mr. Kale was using, checked the analytics associated with the website. Prior to the introduction of the videos, Mr. Kale's website averaged three hits per year. With the videos in place and new videos being added routinely, the web hits skyrocketed to over 3,000 hits per year. With a number that high, Ms. Pickleson realized that it wasn't just Mr. Kale's students who were using the videos; students in other schools around the world were using them as well!

At a staff meeting, Ms. Pickleson shared the numbers with the rest of the faculty and Mr. Kale demonstrated his technique for easy video creation. Other teachers adopted the same or similar versions of the video creation and distribution strategy. Before long, most teachers in the school were posting their class content in the form of videos, multimedia content, or both, for easy student access online.

Mr. Kale, though hesitant at first, was willing to learn and try something new and became a trendsetter before his time. Without knowing what it was called, Mr. Kale had developed a version of a flipped classroom model—a technique of showing videos outside of class, which is now much more widely known and utilized by educators. What started as an accommodation to address the needs of one student with a disability is now a teaching strategy used across the world.

Ms. Lake Keeps Everything

Ms. Lake was a ninth-grade biology teacher, and she had a problem. For years, her biology class ran the same way: Every day, her students arrived to class, and Ms. Lake reviewed material using a slideshow. Ms. Lake held an expectation that the students take notes in a three-ring binder—a school supply she was a big fan of. When she gave the students worksheets, handouts, or any other sheets of paper, she could punch three holes in them and the students could then insert them directly into the binder. There was a comfort in the uniformity that every student would have the same content, presented in the same manner and order, with the ability to review the material in the same way. Then one day, everything changed.

A new student began the school year in Ms. Lake's class, and the student had an accommodation in her IEP stating that she needed to access content digitally. The student was diagnosed with dyslexia and, unfortunately, a cancerous brain tumor. The combination of the tumor, medicinal side effects, and the pre-existing learning disability impacted the student's ability to see and understand content presented to her on paper. Therefore, her IEP team agreed that this student needed all content presented to her digitally in a format that could be magnified and read aloud.

Unsure of how to meet the accommodation and a little nervous that a student wouldn't be using a three-ring binder like everyone else, Ms. Lake turned to the special educators assigned to her school for support. Together, they analyzed the student's needs and found a note-taking tool that the student could use to mimic the paper-based notebook in an accessible digital format. Ms. Lake learned how to scan papers at the copy machine, send them to herself, convert them into text that could be manipulated on the computer, and then share them with the student using a shared drive. Ms. Lake found that the conversion process was only approximately 80 percent accurate on any given worksheet and that she or an educational assistant still needed to manually adjust words and characters. Ultimately, she abandoned the practice in favor of the more expedient process of locating and selecting materials that were already accessible.

Once a resource was located, Ms. Lake needed a way to organize the resource for herself and then share that resource with the student. Being most familiar with the note-taking tool the student was using, Ms. Lake chose to use the same tool for herself. Whenever she found an educational resource, she saved it in the digital note-taking tool. She learned how to tag or label items so that she could keep them organized; and the note-taking tool made this content searchable, shareable, and ubiquitous as well. She found that she didn't need to carry a heavy bag of three-ring binders home with her every night, and she no longer cursed herself for forgetting one of the binders at home or at school. Anywhere she had an internet connection, she had access to her notes.

Ms. Lake then showed the tool to her students, announcing that she was abandoning the use of the three-ring notebook in favor of the new online note-taking tool. She encouraged other students to use the same tool (or something similar) to organize their class notes, and after a few weeks, most students in her classes had adopted the use of the tool too.

AWESOME INSIGHT

Although there are many different digital note-taking tools available, the one Ms. Lake used was Google Keep (keep.google.com). Alternatives to consider would include Microsoft OneNote (onenote.com), Evernote (evernote.com), LiveBinders (livebinders.com), and Diigo (diigo.com).

Ms. Lake went on to present the tool and her strategies for implementation to the entire staff at a faculty meeting, and a few of the teachers followed suit in using it. Then, later in the year, she presented on it at her state educational technology conference.

What started as a necessary accommodation for the executive functioning of one student blossomed into a useful, meaningful approach for many.

Awesome School District Listens Between the Lines

The instructional-technology department of Awesome School District had a problem. They were spending large quantities of time conducting assessments for individual students with learning disabilities, which resulted in the installation and management of the same software for many individual students. Once installed, even more time was spent training the students and staff on how to use the software.

Despite these individualized trainings, Awesome School District was finding that the software was often not being used, either through abandonment or through non-adoption in the first place. The feature that made the software necessary for many students was the ability to have digital text read aloud. Reviewing the research, Awesome School District knew that text-to-speech helped students become better readers; yet for individuals, despite assessments that had recommended the feature and accommodations that had ensured its provision, adoption and implementation rates were still low (Lange, McPhillips, Mulhern, & Wylie, 2006).

Awesome School District recognized that high rates of recommendation and low rates of implementation equaled a problem. Further, they recognized that continuing to conduct assessments that only resulted in a repeated recommendation was inefficient. Armed with this knowledge, they made a decision: they acquired one tool that provided text-to-speech and made it available on every device in the district.

Instead of doing individual trainings with individual educators, they provided mass trainings in multiple formats: online courses, video tutorials, audio recordings, PDF how-tos, and face-to-face trainings. They also conducted trainings directly with the students, where educators and students learned side by side, discussing ways to implement the tool. It still took time, but Awesome School District provided access to the tool to more students in less time and saw a marked increase in usage statistics.

Now, every educator in the district knows to attempt to use the strategy first to see if the universally available tool will meet a student's needs. And documentation of the use of the tool provides further data that can be used when individual needs require further scrutiny.

Today, in Awesome School District, the use of the tool is as commonplace as using the interactive whiteboard software, multimedia slideshow software, and word-processing software. Students help each other learn how to use it, and every educator knows that it is available. A feature now used widely by most was initiated by the necessity of a few.

AWESOME INSIGHT

This video of a TEDx presentation by the author gives practical examples of innovations in widespread educational practice that were originally features used predominantly by people with disabilities: bit.ly/bugajtedx.

The Moral of the Stories

Mr. Kale's, Ms. Lake's, and Awesome School District's stories are indicative of feature matching on a massive scale. Historically, innovations in educational design for everyone start with the mitigation of barriers for someone with a disability. Technologies to help people with disabilities accomplish an otherwise impossible task often turn into productivity tools that are useful for everyone.

At one time, touchscreens were something used exclusively by people who had difficulties controlling a mouse; now, touchscreens are the most common way people interface with devices. Word prediction was a feature originally used exclusively by people with spelling or motor-function difficulties to decrease the number of keystrokes; now, word prediction is offered any time a text message is composed or a web search is performed. Likewise, the now commonplace use of video content in classrooms, access to digital note-taking tools, and availability of text-to-speech functions are just a few more examples of innovative practices born out of the need to supply equal access to a person with a disability.

Warning: One for All
Does Not Eggs-actly Mean All for One

Placing all your eggs in one basket might be the most efficient way to transfer eggs from location to location, but it comes with the risk of losing them all if you drop the basket on the ground. A better plan is to put most of your eggs in one basket and keep one or two others back home, just in case. One inherent danger to the approach of mass feature matching is to assume that the tool you have selected to employ for the masses is the least restrictive tool for every individual. Although the tool might be something to try first, it doesn't necessarily mean it is the least restrictive tool for everyone. Sticking with a tool that isn't meeting a student's needs because it is the readily available tool would be folly and inappropriate.

Educators can fall into the trap of convincing themselves that the tool with which they are most familiar and use most frequently to attempt to solve a problem is always the least restrictive. Knowing how to use a tool and having the experience of seeing it make improvements in the lives of students are strong reasons to attempt to implement that tool first. Still, remain disciplined and deliberate when considering options.

Objective evidence should be a primary factor in considering whether a tool and strategy provided through a mass-feature-matching process is effective for each individual student. Although everyone at the table might want breakfast, only some of the people might like eggs. Whether poached, scrambled, or sunny-side up, if you remember the different ways people like their eggs—and that some people don't like eggs at all—you'll feed everyone who is hungry.

PART IV

ENACTING CHANGE

CHAPTER 11

An Individualized Education Plan for Your Educational Agency

Stan—that guy must be the most intelligent person in all of history. How many times has Stan been asked to reveal his plan? Stan and his plans might be responsible for the bulk of human progress. No matter your position, you can channel your inner Stan to move your educational agency in a positive direction.

Be like Stan and develop a plan.

Individualized Education Programs exist for students to help develop a plan of action to ensure everyone working toward assisting the student is on the same page about what is necessary for learning to take place. If this process works to help students, why not mimic the process to help yourself and your agency grow and change to adopt inclusive and accessible practices too?

Assess what is working by creating a present level of performance for how well your agency is incorporating accessible and inclusive practices. Develop specific, measurable, authentic, realistic, and time-sensitive goals to bring about change and measure growth. Outline actions and those responsible for bringing forth these actions, including people who train others. Then get started on the job of making this vision of change into a reality.

In this chapter, you'll:

1. Learn how to develop a plan of action for issuing forth sustainable change to your education agency regarding inclusive and accessible practices.

2. Explore a method to provide continuous progress for an educational agency analogous to creating an IEP for a student.

ISTE STANDARDS ADDRESSED

ISTE Standards for Educators 1a. Set professional learning goals to explore and apply pedagogical approaches made possible by technology and reflect on their effectiveness.

ISTE Standards for Educators 2a. Shape, advance, and accelerate a shared vision for empowered learning with technology by engaging with education stakeholders.

ISTE Standards for Educators 4a. Dedicate planning time to collaborate with colleagues to create authentic learning experiences that leverage technology.

ISTE Standards for Educators 4d. Demonstrate cultural competency when communicating with students, parents, and colleagues and interact with them as cocollaborators in student learning.

ISTE Standards for Educators 5c. Explore and apply instructional design principles to create innovative digital learning environments that engage and support learning.

Developing a Present Level of (Technology) Performance

Before you run off to make changes here, there, and everywhere, start by evaluating (either alone or with a team) what is working and what is not. In relation to an IEP, this means it is time to create your own present level of functional technology performance.

Using the Quality Indicators as a Needs Assessment

It might be tempting to dive right into the process of developing goals. After all, the word *action* goes in front of the word *plan* for a reason, right? Acting empowers people, and it feels good to get things done.

But don't rush it.

The first step in bringing about change isn't to develop an action plan. Instead, it is to evaluate and measure what's working well and what could be working better. To do so, there need to be honest, nonjudgmental conversations about what is working and what needs to change. Using a rubric to guide the discussion helps keep everyone on task and away from tangents.

The PLAAFP (Present Levels of Academic Achievement and Functional Performance, or present levels) section of the IEP is where educators report assessment results (including those from standardized assessments). Use an impartial rubric to evaluate and measure an educational agency's technology-assistance service-delivery model. One example of such a rubric is the Quality Indicators for Assistive Technology (qiat.org/indicators.html). Rank your agency's performance for each indicator to determine a quantitative score. Scores can be broken down by each indicator to determine which has the greatest need. Using this tool or some version of it, or measuring performance against your own developed rubric, gives you a way to identify which areas to focus on when it comes to the development of goals.

Pop Goes the Bubble and the Bubble Goes Pop

We all live in our own bubbles.

A logical fallacy people tend to adopt is the idea that if one thing happens repeatedly, then it will always happen that way again. This phenomenon is known as the

gambler's fallacy (as explained at YourLogicalFallacyIs.com: yourlogicalfallacyis
.com/the-gamblers-fallacy). If you tossed a coin 10 times and all 10 times it landed
on heads, you might convince yourself that the eleventh time will also be heads.
However, each toss has the same chance of coming up heads. Each chance is independent of the previous flip.

This is how stereotypes are born. For example, if you work with 10 students with
autism who all have trouble regulating behaviors, you might begin to believe that
the eleventh student you work with will also have that same difficulty. Before long,
you might come to believe that every student with autism has difficulty regulating
behavior. But this is false, and we all must remain aware and diligent not to fall into a
similar trap set by the circumstances of our surroundings, especially when assessing
what is working and what is not.

For example, if a policy maker is presented with five cases in a row where a communication device has been broken when going home with the students, that individual
might begin to think that most or all communication devices are likely to break
when they go home. However, when looking at the greater picture and analyzing all
the data, the policy maker might find that 95 other communication devices have also
gone home and have not been damaged. That's a 95 percent success rate of undam-
aged devices!

Exploring beyond our immediate bubble is of utmost importance when assessing
how well your agency is performing on accessible and inclusive design. When
assessing, look beyond the immediate. Look past the house that is on fire right now
to all the houses that aren't currently burning. Don't just look at what is broken; look
at what is working well before making changes.

Developing and Measuring Goals

The process of developing the present levels will likely highlight that your educational agency has some areas that need improvement. But you can't address
everything at once. Which areas are you going to address and in which order?

Listing agency problems and ideas on how to tackle them is a good first step. Choose
an area to address, then generate a list of ideas that might be used to address the
problem. Just keep in mind that ideas can be lofty, general, and not bound by any
amount of time; so this first step is where many educational agencies tend to stop.

Instead, work to develop actionable agency goals—goals that are specific, measurable, achievable, relevant, and limited by time restraints. And agency goals are owned by the people who develop them, leading them to be more invested in them. Like empowering a student to take charge of their own learning, educators work more diligently toward a goal that they've had a hand in designing. Invite them to choose, and you can't lose!

When developing goals, take care to align them with those that already exist in the educational agency. Goals that are synchronized stand a greater chance of gathering support from others in the agency and stand a better chance of success. Once goals are developed, post them for everyone to see, and refer to the goals often. Throughout the year, as new ideas arise, ask if the new ideas work to support the established goals. If the answer is no, then it might not be an idea to pursue at this time.

AWESOME INSIGHT

Although the goal might belong to those who developed it, be wary of surveying the greater populous of educators when developing initiatives. Henry Ford once said that if he had asked people what they wanted, the majority would have said, "Faster horses." It might take an individual or a small group of visionaries to lead the development of the goal to make it something that revolutionizes the culture and has a truly lasting impact.

Duration of Goals

An IEP is intended to be revisited annually (at a minimum) to review, revise, and develop a new or updated plan for the next year. Since goals are typically written to be achieved within a span of one year, write goals with this time frame in mind—but don't stop there. Challenge yourself to develop multiple goals that can be accomplished in one year, and develop at least one goal that can be accomplished within three to five years.

Visionaries plan with the end in mind. Having a long-term vision keeps the team on track through transitions and increases the likelihood of sustaining the changes.

Sample Goals

* By the end of the school year, 90 percent of educators in the educational agency will be designing and implementing 80 percent of their lessons from a project-based learning perspective as measured by administrative observation.

* By the end of the school year, 90 percent of educators in the educational agency will be designing and implementing 80 percent of their lessons using accessible materials as measured by administrative observation.

* By the end of the school year, 90 percent of students in the educational agency will report an 80 percent increase in their enjoyment level of the school experience as measured by quantitative survey reports.

* By the end of year three, 90 percent of IEP teams will contact an accessible-design facilitator prior to the IEP meeting to discuss the provision of assistance as measured by data collected per request.

Stay Focused

If you work in education long enough, you'll see a pattern emerge in which every few years, there seems to be a new initiative or piece of technology implemented. Sometimes the item is brought in to replace an outdated system; sometimes the item is introduced to resolve a problem that a population of students is experiencing; and sometimes, sadly, the item is put in place to satiate the whim of someone who just liked it better and thought it would be a good idea. Jumping from item to item and initiative to initiative every few years can be frustrating for everyone involved.

When afloat on an ocean as big as technology, it's easy to want to drift around forever, nibbling at every morsel that looks tasty. Don't be tempted to bite on every new item that promises to solve your problems. There is a sea of people out there with things to sell that promise solutions. Without some sort of plan, you could be lost at sea forever.

Develop a goal, and stick to that goal. Measure progress, and revise when necessary. Create a new goal when it's time. Do this, and you'll successfully navigate your course, finding your way to your destination (and without falling overboard!).

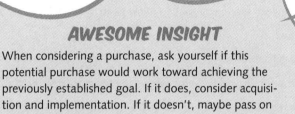

AWESOME INSIGHT

When considering a purchase, ask yourself if this potential purchase would work toward achieving the previously established goal. If it does, consider acquisition and implementation. If it doesn't, maybe pass on it for now, because it might serve as a distraction from achieving the desired outcome.

SEEKING NORY

"Nory, don't touch that! It's not safe!" shouted Marvin. The two fish stared at the shimmering beacon of light.

"But it's so shiny. Look at it there, glistening in the water. I want it so badly!" Nory exclaimed. "It is so tempting …"

"No—don't! It's a trap! It's just trying to hook you—don't be fooled! Don't bite!"

"No, no. Look at it. All glittery and gold, shining in front of me. How can anything so pretty be dangerous? It wants to help us. It wants me to adopt it. In fact, 'it' is 'he,' and his name is Shiny. And Shiny *will* be mine!" stated Nory, with confidence and gumption.

"Nory! Don't!!"

"Too late! I'm touching it!"

"Nory, no!!!"

GULP!

"Great. Are you happy now? We've been eaten. Now we're inside this thing. You were lured in—you fell for the bait. And now we're stuck here, likely to be digested for all of eternity. We're never getting out! We're going to *die* in here!"

"Oops! Sorry! I thought I was doing a good thing. I didn't know. It looked harmless…" explained Nory.

Something green waving in the water caught Marvin's eye. "Wait! Look there's some seaweed stuck on a tooth. Quick! Grab it, and we'll tickle our way out!"

"Like this?"

"Yes! Wiggle it!"

The fish were sloshed up and down as the beast tried to resist chuckling.

"I think it's working. Keep it up!" bellowed Marvin. "The mouth is opening. Quick! Swim for it!"

Nory's tiny blue tailfin fluttered. "I'm a-comin'!"

Both fish exploded out of the mouth in a flurry of bubbles.

"Phew! We made it! Nory, we made it!!! Nory … Nory?"

"Look! There's another one! It's so shiny—I want this one too. Come here, little shiny thing. You *will* be mine!"

"Oh no! Not again…" Marvin said, grabbing his best friend by the dorsal and pulling her away. "This little morsel is not for eating."

Now, Next, Later, Never

After goals have been developed, it might seem like the next step is to outline the specific steps necessary to achieve them. The fun, exciting, and empowering part of developing an action plan is developing the first steps—planning and actually *doing* things feels good! But resist the temptation to start with a list of to-do items.

The first—and much more difficult step—is to have the conversation about what to *stop* doing. Which actions and activities are happening right now that aren't contributing to the established goals? Stopping is harder than starting; it takes honesty, courage, and strength to admit that what's happening might not be the most efficient or effective use of time. Make a list of items to stop doing and, once complete, start on the list of things to do instead.

Action Steps

The goals have been drafted. You know the change that you want to see happen. You've outlined what isn't working and what you need to stop doing. Now, it is time to get down to the nitty-gritty. What, exactly, are you going to do instead? What are the specific action steps necessary to make accomplishing the goal a reality? For a student, these might be called "services." For example, a speech-language pathologist is going to meet with a student 60 minutes a week to work on the goals outlined in the IEP. The service outlines who is going to do what and how often. When drafting the steps for your agency, specifically carve out who is going to do each specific item and establish specific deadlines.

These action steps were developed by educators and represent what could be done to begin bringing about accessible practices in your educational agency.

Sample Action Steps

* Once a month for the entire school year, starting in August, accessible-design facilitators will share on social media how an educational experience designer used at least one piece of technology to improve accessibility.

* By the end of September, a member of the assistive-technology team will meet at least once with the director of special education to discuss the creation of a position focused on supporting educators' consideration of technology to design accessible educational experiences.

* By the end of October, the director of special education will meet at least once to collaborate with related service personnel regarding the development of an accessible-design-service delivery model.

* By the end of November, an accessible-design facilitator will create a social bookmarking feed displayed on the agency website, and each accessible-design facilitator will post to it biweekly about accessibility for the remainder of the school year.

- By the end of December, an accessible-design facilitator will duplicate the content from the slide decks of two existing face-to-face professional development offerings into an online, on-demand format.

- By the end of January, an accessible-design facilitator will meet with administrators at three different schools to develop a list of action items to promote a least restrictive option initiative at their school.

- By the end of February, an educational experience designer will design and implement at least three model lessons from a Project-Based Learning perspective in one classroom that has a population of at least three students with a disability.

- By the end of March, a team of three accessible-design facilitators will create a list of resources that offer educators accessible and open-sourced educational materials.

- By the end of April, each accessible-design facilitator will participate in at least three agency-level committee meetings pertaining to the acquisition of agency-wide materials.

- By the end of May, each accessible-design facilitator will create at least three new professional-development experiences pertaining to accessible design.

- By the end of June, a team of three accessible-design facilitators will create an inventory of every support item in our agency and report on the status (available, out with student, or broken) of each item.

- By the end July, an educational experience designer, with support from an accessible-design facilitator, will create an infographic for next year's least-restrictive-option initiative.

Analyzing and Reporting Success

Throughout the course of the plan, collect data on how a student is progressing toward previously established goals. Periodically (biannually or quarterly) analyze the data being collected toward your established service-delivery goals and adjust accordingly.

Do you need to do more of something? Do you need to do less of something? Do you need to just maintain the current course to hit your target? Trust the numbers, not your gut or ego. Numbers are impartial—they don't care if you meet your goals or not. You can trust them to give you accurate information which you can use to make better decisions. Then make the necessary changes to make progress toward the goals. With sustained effort, you'll succeed!

No one will know what you accomplished unless you tell them. Provide reports to the necessary stakeholders about your achievements. These stakeholders might be local school administrators, agency administrators, or anyone else who influences or impacts service delivery. Advertising successes and sharing progress keeps people informed about the work you've done and increases people's support for ongoing endeavors. Don't be shy! It isn't bragging; it's sharing!

Reports should reflect the goals that have been established, highlight the actions taken to meet the goals, and then identify the outcomes. Use multiple modalities such as videos, infographics, slide decks, and charts to share the results.

After taking a moment to celebrate a job well done, it's time to get back to work. Review the data you collected to develop the next present level of performance, craft new goals, and implement new actions. Begin the process again to maintain and sustain ongoing progress.

CHAPTER 12

Effective Professional Development

One of the areas addressed in the Quality Indicators for Assistive Technology (QIAT) is professional development. Invariably, some actions will involve the training of others. Professional development is necessary to make change happen.

Educational experience designers are constantly learning new things. They model for students that learning is a lifelong endeavor. Accessible-design facilitators coach students and educational experience designers on how to select and implement technology that works to meet their objectives. This can be read from two perspectives: The first involves your learning. To make the most out of every experience, focus your time to make it purposeful, drive yourself forward on the path toward educational enlightenment, and then share your experiences to cultivate a culture of change. The second involves providing insights on how to issue forth this change in others by creating inclusive practices through technology and offering effective, enjoyable, and meaningful training.

Accessible-design facilitators and other champions of accessibility are ultimately crafters of professional-development experiences. They become educational experience designers for adults. While reading this chapter, think about how the content can aid your own learning and how you can then use it to provide professional development to others.

In this chapter, you'll:

1.   Explore a mindset for seeking out learning opportunities.

2.   Examine how to break down professional-development opportunities into a series of microtransactions rather than large events.

3.   Learn how offering and designing adult educational experiences that use multiple modalities helps reach the widest range of needs.

ISTE STANDARDS ADDRESSED

ISTE Standards for Educators 1a. Set professional learning goals to explore and apply pedagogical approaches made possible by technology and reflect on their effectiveness.

ISTE Standards for Educators 1b. Pursue professional interests by creating and actively participating in local and global learning networks.

ISTE Standards for Educators 1c. Stay current with research that supports improved student-learning outcomes, including findings from the learning sciences.

ISTE Standards for Educators 2a. Shape, advance, and accelerate a shared vision for empowered learning with technology by engaging with education stakeholders.

ISTE Standards for Educators 2c. Model for colleagues the identification, exploration, evaluation, curation, and adoption of new digital resources and tools for learning.

ISTE Standards for Educators 3a. Create experiences for learners to make positive, socially responsible contributions and to exhibit empathetic behavior online that builds relationships and community.

ISTE Standards for Educators 4a. Dedicate planning time to collaborate with colleagues to create authentic learning experiences that leverage technology.

ISTE Standards for Educators 4d. Demonstrate cultural competency when communicating with students, parents, and colleagues and interact with them as cocollaborators in student learning.

ISTE Standards for Educators 5a. Use technology to create, adapt, and personalize learning experiences that foster independent learning and accommodate learner differences and needs.

ISTE Standards for Educators 5b. Design authentic learning activities that align with content-area standards, and use digital tools and resources to maximize active, deep learning.

ISTE Standards for Educators 6a. Foster a culture where students take ownership of their learning goals and outcomes in both independent and group settings.

ISTE Standards for Educators 6b. Manage the use of technology and student learning strategies in digital platforms, virtual environments, hands-on makerspaces, and/or in the field.

ISTE Standards for Educators 6c. Create learning opportunities that challenge students to use a design process and computational thinking to innovate and solve problems.

ISTE Standards for Educators 6d. Model and nurture creativity and creative expression to communicate ideas, knowledge, and/or connections.

ISTE Standards for Educators 7a. Provide alternative ways for students to demonstrate competency and reflect on their learning by using technology.

Developing the Right Mindset for Success

Let's play a word-association game. You yell out the first word that pops into your head when you hear a term. (Don't worry. No one will look at you funny if you pull your head out of this book and shout out a word. Just try it!)

Ready? Here's the term: *professional development.*

The word that likely popped into your mind and that you so boldly yelled out was *boring.* But the word *professional* need not be a synonym for *boring.* Wouldn't it be better if the professional-development experiences you were engaged didn't feel like taking foul-tasting medicine? Wouldn't it be better if you enjoyed the experience while also learning from it?

Beyond your own learning, if you're responsible for training others—you're an educational experience designer for adults. And adults want to avoid the pain and suffering brought about by boredom just as much as kids do! If people enjoy the professional-development experience, they'll be more likely to remember the content delivered during the training and be motivated to put the strategies in place.

Learning, no matter your age, should be fun! Educational experience designers, accessible-design facilitators, and every other educator should be the best learners and exhibit joy in the learning process. There is a never-ending well of information, strategies, tools, and resources waiting to be experienced; and learning new stuff is what education is all about! Each day provides a fresh opportunity to learn a new technology, principle, or perspective to fulfill the promise of providing inclusive educational experiences for all. The first step is adopting the Growth Mindset for yourself and realizing that you yourself can change for the better, given enough time, applied effort, and positive attitude.

Combat Cognitive Dissonance

Cognitive dissonance is a term used to describe that awkward phenomenon of being faced with evidence that comes into conflict with what we've come to believe to be true. It attempts to rob us of our ability to look at facts impartially, empirically, and objectively; it works to keep us stuck. Luckily, cognitive dissonance can be overcome! Once aware of its negative impact and influence, a person can use this awareness to hold fast to the principles of logic.

Embrace a mindset that allows you to be open to learning new things and recognizing that what you hold true today can and should change when the evidence demands it. *Seek out that change.* Be open to the possibility that what you know to be true now might not always be your truth. Always be willing to let fact, evidence, and logic dictate your beliefs and actions. Do not succumb to the temptations of your ego! Resist, and let knowledge and wisdom be your reward!

Crush Confirmation Bias

A close cousin to cognitive dissonance is the concept of confirmation bias. *Confirmation bias* is the notion that what you're doing is right simply because you're the one doing it. It manifests itself by ignoring evidence contrary to what you have established to be true and by only seeking out evidence that supports your own established claim. Confirmation bias exists within people to help them avoid the ugly, awkward feeling brought about by cognitive dissonance.

Educational experience designers and accessible-design facilitators actively seek to keep themselves aware of confirmation bias. Reading research, analyzing facts, and absorbing new ideas with an open mind helps one to objectively see all sides of an issue. When new information clashes with prior knowledge, those aware of these psychological phenomena can actively fight to form conclusions, make decisions, and take actions using the most sound, logical judgments.

AWESOME INSIGHT

Keep a record, either publicly or privately, that documents your growth over time. When you have an insight or reach a conclusion about a topic, start with the phrase, "I used to think," and insert your previous thoughts on a topic. Then add "But now I think" and describe how new evidence has altered your thinking. This type of self-reflection can bring about personal growth and change.

Make Learning Intentional, Not Incidental

Carrying laundry upstairs is not the same as doing burpees. Sure, both are forms of exercise, but bringing your clothes to your bedroom happens out of necessity, with much less caloric burn than dropping up and down as part of a focused fitness routine.

Humans are constantly taking in information; just by being awake, people learn. But this is *incidental* learning, and it is not the same as applying mental energy to becoming more knowledgeable about (or skilled in) a specific subject. Like the idea of developing an intentional fitness practice, making your learning purposeful and intentional (versus incidental or accidental) leads to far more effective results.

As a professional, the responsibility of learning something new falls directly on you and no one else. Don't wait for training to be thrust upon you. Instead, decide what you'd like to learn about technology, inclusion, and accessible design and then take the initiative to learn it. Be the person who asks, "How can I learn this?" versus the person who says, "No one ever taught me this." Say, "I can learn how!" versus "I'm not trained to do that." When you invest time in learning about a topic in which you are passionate, it won't feel like work at all. Few experiences in life are as fulfilling as studying a topic you love and applying that knowledge to solve a problem that helps others.

Setting and Achieving Professional-Development Goals

Let's do a little exercise. Take a moment to list some things you'd like to learn more about. (Here's a little area to write your list, but don't feel obligated to use it. If you'd rather use a mind-mapping, digital note-taking, or list-making tool, go for it. The box is just an option.)

Now, brainstorm! Put down everything and anything that comes to your mind—don't hold anything back. At this stage, there are no bad ideas. What do you want to know more about? *Go!*

Okay, got your list? Now, it's time to prioritize. Which items are the most pressing? Which will have the greatest impact on you and the people you serve? Which, if you learned it, would bring you the most satisfaction and happiness? That's your focus. That's where you spend your time. That's where you begin.

But there's another step—a harder step: turning these ideas into measurable, time-constrained goals. Like a goal written for a student's IEP, take a moment to generate a professional learning goal for yourself.

Don't share your goal with anyone. Research suggests that the act of sharing your personal goal decreases your likelihood of achieving it (Gollwitzer, Sheeran, Michalski, & Seifert, 2009). The idea is that when you share your goals, your trick your brain into thinking you've achieved your goals and, therefore, don't follow through with the action steps necessary to really achieve them. Like Gandalf said to Frodo when he gave him the One Ring to Rule Them All: "Keep it secret. Keep it safe." Unlike shared agency goals, which you want to post and share everywhere for all to see, your personal goal is *your* goal. When you achieve it, you can scream it from the rooftops if you like. But for now, mum's the word, okay?

Now, there's one more step, and it's the hardest of all: You must *do it*. Day in and day out, you must spend time on achieving the goal. You must stick to it *every day*, making decisions that steer you toward progress. Just remember: nothing feels quite as good as achieving a goal.

Engaging Participants In Their Professional Development

Professional development, at a staff meeting or a workshop, doesn't need to be a one-way flow of information. Project-Based Learning, Growth Mindset, and Universal Design for Learning don't just work for those who are school-aged; they work for everyone. No matter your role, if you are creating an educational experience for others, use these practices to engage, enlighten, and empower participants.

Applying Project-Based Learning to PD

Consider inviting participants to outline a professional-development (PD) problem or present them with a PD problem to solve. Ask them to develop goals and an action plan to solve it, and then invite participants to share the technology they know to address the problem. Expand and expound upon these moments by sharing your own insights into how the known technology could be applied to help in the situation. Introduce new solutions as well, helping the participants learn new technologies and/or new ways of thinking. Collaborative professional development based on authentic problems is more engaging, empowering, and effective at bringing about lasting change to a system.

 THE PRINCESS OF PROJECT-BASED PD

Once upon a time, a king ruled a land. Court was held once a month, where his nobles would gather to listen to him make proclamations and laws. The king was neither cruel nor corrupt. He was fair-minded and benevolent; and he tried his best to keep his kingdom peaceful and prosperous.

The burden, however, proved to be too great. For no one can make correct decisions all the time. Even those with the best of intentions fail sometimes. Troubled and dismayed by his missteps, the king eventually slipped into a depression. Stressed and despondent, he abdicated the throne, bequeathing it to his daughter, who could no longer bear to see her father in such misery.

The princess applied a different approach to ruling the kingdom. During court, she asked the nobles to outline the problems of the land and had them prioritize these problems. After the list was generated, she invited them to split up the problems based on what each noble felt was most important. Then they attempted to develop potential solutions to the problem most important to them.

The princess, commanding respect and competence, guided the conversations, asking probing questions and resolving disputes as needed. When potential solutions were ready, the princess asked each group of nobles to present the solutions to the others, and then, to the people who lived in their fiefdoms.

Together, action plans were formed to turn potential solutions into actual ones. The people and their leaders felt a sense of propriety over the solutions and worked even harder to make them a reality. Due to the wisdom and willingness of one princess, who trusted her people to chart their own course and steer their own ship, the kingdom changed for the better forever.

An Example of Problem-Based PD

Technology-resource teachers who function as instructional facilitators attended a workshop to learn about a new literacy support tool, Read&Write for Windows. Instead of going through the software feature by feature, function by function, click by agonizing click, they were given a 10-minute overview of the purpose of the software and shown how to locate operational tutorials. They were then presented with four scenarios, with each scenario detailing authentic situations in which a student or educator was having difficulty. They were told the software could help, but it was up to them to figure out potential solutions.

The scenarios were as follows:

Scenario 1. You are working with a teacher to plan lessons on the topics of science, social studies, or both. The teacher provides study guides for the students to review before, after, and during the lessons. However, the study guides are primarily text, and the reading level might be too high for some of the students in the class. What tools and strategies (including features of Read&Write for Windows) are available to help this teacher?

Scenario 2. Rocco is a voracious reader and can verbally answer any question you throw at him. However, he struggles when it comes to writing these responses, including written tests. He gets frustrated with spelling and writing his thoughts in any form, including typed. What tools and strategies (including features of Read&Write for Windows) are available to help this student?

Scenario 3. Shannon has a project due. She is going to research information on polar bears, develop a plan of action for how to protect their environment, and send her results to scientists working to preserve habitats. Before writing the report, she needs to gather and organize some facts. What tools and strategies (including features of Read&Write for Windows) are available to help this student?

Scenario 4. Tanya has access to a computer with text-to-speech available as a function, but her teacher won't give up his use of paper. Every lesson involves reading a block of text on a piece of paper and answering some questions pertaining to that block of text. Tanya, however, is struggling to read the directions, the blocks of text, and the questions. What tools and strategies (including features of Read&Write for Windows) are available to help this student (and teacher)?

Throughout the session, the accessible-design facilitators moved about the room, discussing the scenarios, answering questions, and providing guidance. Near the end of the experience, the whole group reassembled to discuss solutions. The participants proved to be up to the task, met the challenge, and found solutions beyond what the designers of the workshop even intended or expected. They not only learned the functions and features of the software but found solutions to common problems experienced by those they serve. When the workshop was complete, the technology-resource teachers returned to their schools emboldened with the confidence and experience of how to implement the features of the software.

Hiding the Medicine in the Brownies

People can't learn from a professional-development experience if they don't attend or participate in it. One strategy to entice participants into signing up for a professional-development workshop is to title the session in such a way that it speaks to solving the problem plaguing potential participants.

For example, imagine a session about minimizing the use of paper in a classroom in favor of digital tools due to the increased accessibility those tools might offer. This session might be titled, "Making Your Content Accessible to All Learners," but that doesn't necessarily call out to the daily frustrations of a general educator. Participants who would consider attending a workshop with this title might already have an interest in making content accessible, such as a special-education case manager who is tasked with retrofitting inaccessible materials. Many general educators would likely regard this session as "not for them"—not because they don't care about the topic but because they don't recognize accessibility as a problem in their classroom.

Consider a different title, such as "How to Never Stand in Line at the Copy Machine Again." Standing in line for the copy machine and wrestling with paper jams has been the bane of every educator. The description for the session could be written to appeal to the desires of educators everywhere who want to be more efficient, buying themselves more time. Once people are in the door, the strategy shifts to having them participate in an experience that solves their problem as well as the one you were hoping to solve by offering the workshop in the first place.

In the session, wrap the content that supports your own goal around the content important to the participant. In this way, meaningful context is provided to the learner while tapping into their prior knowledge. For example, in the same session about accessibility, consider showing off a tool familiar to most educators, such as Kahoot (kahoot.com), a tool used for formative assessments. Encourage those familiar with the tool to share their experiences with it and whether or not they consider it worthy of the time investment of others. Then explore the tool further from the perspective of accessibility. Ask the group questions that lead them to realize that during a session of Kahoot, the students who are still learning how to decode words on the screen in the front of the room might have trouble quickly answering a question with accuracy. When designing the educational experience, consider hiding the medicine in the brownies to help people get better without them knowing they were being treated in the first place.

AWESOME INSIGHT

If you just can't think of a clever title that also solves a problem for potential participants, stick to naming the session based on what the tool does rather than the tool itself. For example, use titles like "Strategies to Improve Reading and Writing Abilities" not "Using Snap&Read Universal." Highlight the function of a tool to get at the heart of whatever problem people are looking to solve for themselves.

Achieving Sustainable Change through Consistent Actions

The Grand Canyon is one of the seven natural wonders of the world—one of the most amazing sites anyone can behold. How was the Grand Canyon formed? It wasn't a giant meteor impacting the earth that caused this majestic destination. Instead, it was molecule after molecule of water gradually wearing away rock and stone to form a deep, winding chasm worthy of breathtaking awe. It often takes time filled with repetitive work before something wonderful can be forged.

Lasting change will not happen immediately. Whether building an individual PD plan for yourself or for your agency, plan to be like the water in the Grand Canyon; plan for a series of events that work toward meeting your goal by complementing and building upon one another. Over time, change *will* occur, and you'll have built something inspiring and long lasting, just like the Grand Canyon.

The Super Bowl Shuffle

Millions of viewers from around the world watch the spectacle of the Super Bowl. And with that many eyeballs on one event, marketers rush to put their best advertisements forward. Super Bowl commercials have become just as much a part of the event as the game itself. But what's the logic and strategy behind spending many millions of dollars on 30 to 60 seconds of airtime? Advertisers don't expect people to run out to buy their product the second it is displayed in the commercial. Instead, the advertisers are playing the long game.

The hope is that during some future shopping trip, people (*lots* of people) will pick up the product. Consciously or unconsciously, the advertisers hope their ad will influence people enough to drop some cash on their product. This means that companies must be patient to see a return on their investment. When it comes to advertising, there is no such thing as instant gratification.

Learning about a new tool, strategy, or approach is like advertising a product during the Super Bowl and beyond. One shouldn't have the expectation that a tool, strategy, or other support will be adopted or implemented immediately. It will likely take time for an educator to adopt and integrate something new. Therefore, persistence, consistency, and a continuous supply of evidence that the change or support is worth the time investment is what will ultimately prove to be successful in issuing forth sustainable change.

The Rule of 22

When you hear about a good television show for the first time, do you immediately run home to check it out? How about a new book mentioned by a friend? A new recipe? Musical artist? Restaurant? Anything?

It is usually not until you've heard about something from multiple people multiple times that the idea to explore that thing seeps into your consciousness. People typically need things repeated before taking action. People typically need things repeated before taking action. People typically need things repeated before taking action.

This phenomenon holds true for educators when they hear about a new resource for the first time. No matter how great a conference, workshop, session, or training might have been, educators are busy people. Investing the time it takes to explore a new tool needs to come with some assurance that it will be worth it. That assurance often comes after hearing it works from other people. There will always be early adopters, but even the early adopters of one resource can be late adopters of another. There are just too many resources available (and new ones keep popping up all the time)!

As an accessible-design facilitator (or in any position where your responsibility is to share resources, train, or coach others), delayed or late adoption can try your patience. After all, your time is limited as well. If you go somewhere and suggest an idea to an educator, it seems reasonable for that educator to perhaps try what was suggested, right?

Wrong.

It might take multiple experiences before the educator considers a resource valuable enough to implement it. With the best of intentions, the educator may want to implement a resource, but other, more pressing items pop up. Meanwhile, time marches on. Before long, that resource, which might have seemed great at the time, phased into the background as it slipped off the priority list. But remember: "not right now" does not mean "not ever."

Repeated experiences with multiple nonadopters can leave anyone wondering what they are doing wrong. Perhaps what is being done wrong is not providing the options enough times or in enough modalities. Perhaps the targeted educators haven't heard the strategy enough times and/or in enough ways. What if what they really need is to hear it more times? If that is true, then the key to influence is persistence and patience.

How many times does it take before you or anyone with whom you share resources and ideas investigates, implements, and successfully adopts a new resource? What is the magic number?

Perhaps it is 22.

As a professional developer, adopt a philosophy of creating opportunities for any given educator to hear, see, or otherwise experience a strategy at least 22 times before becoming frustrated with the situation. When a person does not immediately adopt a support, simply say, "Well, I guess the person hasn't gotten to 22 yet! I guess I need to keep plugging away!" Challenge yourself to provide the resource, intervention, or strategy again in another way (as many times and ways as necessary) until the educator takes action.

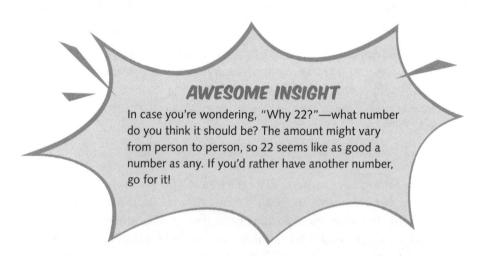

AWESOME INSIGHT

In case you're wondering, "Why 22?"—what number do you think it should be? The amount might vary from person to person, so 22 seems like as good a number as any. If you'd rather have another number, go for it!

Microtransactions as PD

How do mobile games like Candy Crush and Pokémon Go make money when the apps are free to play? The answer is an economic philosophy known as *microtransactions*. The idea is predicated on the notion that people are willing to spend less money more frequently than more money all at once. Rather than charging for the game, these app developers charge for enhancements to the game. By removing the barrier to entry, the app developers are banking on the idea that people will actually spend more money over time if they are invited to pay small amounts each time. So far, it seems to be working out for a lot of these companies!

Getting to 22 seems like it would take a long time. Who has 22 opportunities to present ideas to the same person? But what if we applied the microtransaction philosophy to professional development? Since investing an hour or more can seem like a lot of time to participants, what if they were offered the opportunity to learn in short (micro) bursts of time instead? What if PD was re-envisioned to be considered something other than open-ended investments in larger blocks of time?

When thought of from this microcontent perspective, reaching 22 opportunities to share information or present content might not seem so daunting. What follows are a series of ways to provide microtransactions of information as a form of professional development, though this list is nowhere near inclusive. What innovative ways can you use to share and gather information, insights, and perspectives?

Email Signatures

Everyone uses email. Create a signature that has more than your contact information and credentials. Many people put inspiring quotes that reference a perspective they share or a thought they want to convey. Consider adding a link to a resource as well. Each email message sent is an opportunity to add a tick toward 22.

Away Messages

You can be sharing a resource even when you're absent. Set up an away message with a brief explanation and a link to a resource you want everyone to know about. This way, even when you're sick or on vacation, you can help others get to 22.

Social Media

Twitter, Facebook, Pinterest, Instagram, SnapChat, Voxer, or any tool that allows you to share bite-sized pieces of information can educate others about relevant topics. Images (including memes), videos (including gifs), audio files (including podcasts), and links to other forms of media can be included to help deliver an effective message. Every post is an opportunity for others to climb the ladder toward 22.

Public and Social Bookmarking

Resources accumulate like snowflakes in a blizzard. Organizing them so you can quickly find them again is imperative to maintaining an efficient practice. Social bookmarking tools such as Diigo allow a user to tag resources in a way that makes them easy to find again. When needed, users can search tags to quickly locate resources they've previously found.

This archive of resources can be maintained privately or publicly. When made public, educators can search your archive for resources too. An account of online bookmarks can be maintained individually or by multiple accounts in a group. (Social bookmarking occurs when a number of individuals share resources within a group.) Instead of searching the entire internet for a resource, educators seeking assistance have the valuable option to search this smaller, vetted repository. Maintaining a social bookmarking group and promoting its use to educators empowers educators with another way to reach 22.

Strategy-a-Day Methodologies

Stalagmites and stalactites form gradually as each drip of water rolls off the ceiling of a cave and leaves behind molecules of sediment. As the years roll by, drop by drop, a unique and beautiful structure is formed. Creating a methodology for educators to accumulate knowledge daily is like being that constant drip of water.

A strategy-a-day calendar, blog, email group, or other such daily posts are tools that can be created to consistently pepper educators with resources (see Figure 12.1). At minimum, a strategy-a-day methodology serves as an awareness tool that brings new information to educators.

Each year, leaders of educational agencies create initiatives that work to meet over-arching goals. Examples might be a push to implement core vocabulary principles for students with language disorders, to use literacy software to support reading, to apply positive behavior protocols, or to shift toward Project-Based Learning. Strategy-a-day methods can act as a catalyst to whatever initiative is being carried out. Strategies that support the initiative can be placed at periodic (or aperiodic) intervals throughout the body of the resource. Those engaging in the strategy-a-day resource are then provided a consistent reminder of the whys and hows of an initiative. Over time, these methods issue forth a successful implementation of the initiative—and change happens! When putting together a strategy-a-day resource, meet the challenge to reference the initiative at least 22 times to bring forth the lasting change.

Figure 12.1 Loudoun County Public School's strategy-a-day calendar.

To create a crowd-sourced, strategy-a-day resource, invite stakeholders such as educational experience designers, accessible-design facilitators, related service personnel, administrators, other educators, and students to document their favorite strategy in a shared location, like a Google Forms or Google Slides presentation. The request could invite stakeholders to share the top five strategies, resources, or ideas they wish every other person knew. The more people are participating and contributing, the less work it will be for the individuals putting the resource together.

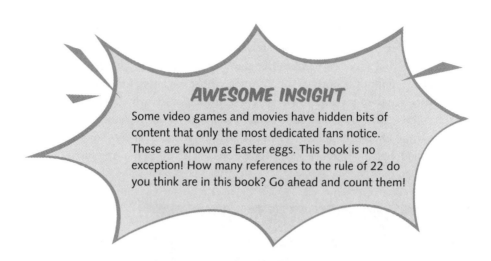

AWESOME INSIGHT

Some video games and movies have hidden bits of content that only the most dedicated fans notice. These are known as Easter eggs. This book is no exception! How many references to the rule of 22 do you think are in this book? Go ahead and count them!

Multiple Means of Successful PD

Just like students in school, adult learners have their preferences. People might prefer to get content via video, audio, imagery, text, face-to-face interaction, online, and/or any number of other types of delivery methodologies. Therefore, delivering content via a single or solitary modality means you are knowingly leaving out a subset of people who might otherwise utilize that content.

Once you've designed an educational experience, consider replicating the experience using a differing modality. Before creating something new, create something again in a different modality. If you did a webinar, share the audio via podcast; if you made a podcast, create a text file as a transcript; if you created a how-to video, create a step-by-step guide that explains that same content. Then organize and share every modality with your constituents. By offering them choices, you can ensure you are meeting most people's—if not everyone's—needs.

When creating these multiple modalities, you don't necessarily have to start from scratch. Read on to discover some shortcuts and other good ideas to help you produce large quantities of quality content.

Replicate Yourself

In the comedy classic *Multiplicity*, Michael Keaton replicates himself to enjoy more time to himself. Of course, it all goes horribly wrong, and he learns that the best way to enjoy life is to appreciate every part of it—the good and the bad. But just because things didn't work out for Michael Keaton's character in the movie doesn't mean he didn't have a good idea. With modern technology, one can successfully and cheaply replicate oneself!

Right now, someone is watching a TED talk and learning awesome ideas from the individual giving the talk. At the same time, someone else might be reading a blog post by that same presenter, and yet another someone might be listening to a podcast episode featuring that same presenter. A fourth person might be talking with the author in person. All four experiences might be happening simultaneously and might even involve discussion of the same content. In this way, the author can be in more than one place at one time! The author has successfully replicated himself, and you can do the same!

When creating professional-development experiences for others, keep this fact in mind: If it can be recorded, record it; and if it can be shared, share it. Creating online, openly shared content allows more people access at any given moment. When you start to plan your next PD workshop, consider spending some of that time asking what gives you the best return on your time investment. By all means, plan face-to-face workshop experiences, but also consider how the learning can be replicated by those not in attendance; then step into the replicator and push the button! Each time you push it, you add another opportunity for someone else to eek closer toward 22. And each time someone else climbs inside and pushes it, you have an opportunity to eek closer to 22!

Premade Modules

Don't have time to create a customized training experience for educators? No worries! A variety of ready-to-use modules exist from different organizations and companies. These online, self-paced, straightforward experiences can provide just the right amount of refreshment. Use these modules to refill your own Cup of Knowledge, and invite others to take a sip as well. Benefit from the time spent by those who developed these content-rich modules to reach the magical 22. Table 12.1 shows examples of existing training.

Table 12.1 Training Modules for Educators

Module	Description
Autism Internet Modules (AIM) from the Ohio Center for Autism and Low Incidence (OCALI) (autisminternetmodules.org)	Designed for anyone who supports, instructs, works with, or lives with someone with autism
Assistive Technology Internet Modules (ATIM) from the Ohio Center for Autism and Low Incidence (atinternetmodules.org)	Designed for anyone who supports, instructs, works with, or lives with someone who has a disability
Modules Addressing Special Education and Teacher Education (MAST) from East Carolina University (mast.ecu.edu/picker.php)	Designed with broad-application concepts for all educators working with students with disabilities; formatted to be completed in approximately one hour
Dynamic Learning Maps (DLM) Professional Development (dlmpd.com)	Focuses on math and literacy strategies for those working with students with significant cognitive disabilities
POWER ACC Modules developed by PaTTAN (Pennsylvania Training and Technical Assistance Network) with Gail Van Tatenhove (bit.ly/poweraacmodules)	Meant to improve communication skills by providing flexible, generative vocabulary for students who need or use augmentative/alternative communication
Texthelp Product Training (bit.ly/texthelptrainingportal)	Provides complete tutorials to answer questions related to Texthelp products

Seed Communities

Be part of a community whose members share the same vested interest. If a community does not exist around the interest, it is your responsibility to create one. Find a platform that might work to meet the largest number of community members, invite a few people who share the interest to join, and then commit to posting information to that forum consistently. Pose open-ended questions to spur interactions and exchanges. Generate questions that allow people to share their experiences, and keep at it! Community building takes time and can seem fruitless at first. But with some tender loving care, it will blossom.

When the community begins to take shape, the fruits of your labor will become apparent. Eventually, the organism will flourish and generate its own seeds.

Members will start to ask their own questions, and the community will propagate. The role of progenitor will give way to that of moderator.

Once a community has been formed, relationships grow, and its members harvest learning from one another. When a community exists, learning happens. The learning that results from community involvement may have started as a direct way to reach 22. When the community is established and self-perpetuating, it becomes an indirect method for reaching 22, taking no additional time from the creator.

Join Research Clubs

It's time to party! Slap on your sexy shoes. Grab your fancy outfit. Tonight, we're going out! It's time to paint the town *read!* We're going clubbing at the newest, hottest rager in the city! It's Club Research—that place where people drink facts like it's happy hour!

Everyone heading to the club comes prepared, having read and summarized one research article related to a shared topic of interest. Maybe they're research articles on using augmentative/alternative communication for language development, studies on how to improve reading abilities, journal reviews on a proven methodology for helping students construct coherent thoughts using text, or any other topic relevant to contemporary educational practices. Clubgoers get together and share their summaries of an article before, during, or after dancing the night away. And discussions on the implications of the research can carry on into the wee hours of the next morning.

When the party is over, everyone will leave with happy memories of the good times they had out on the town and feel satisfied that they are keeping informed with the latest research in their field of practice. Perhaps participation in a research-club experience will be a few additional rungs on the ladder toward 22.

Connect at Conferences

Much of what can be learned can be learned online. But all the content in the world cannot replicate the experience of what can be gained by attending and presenting at face-to-face, local, regional, national, or international conferences.

Imagine dating someone online and never meeting them in person. You need that face-to-face experience to know for sure if that person is "The One." Connecting with people in person solidifies relationships that may have been started virtually, and attending conferences provides an opportunity to learn from people who aren't prolific in digital spaces.

AWESOME INSIGHT

Perspectives are not research. A blog post or social media discussion on a subject is not the same thing as a criterion-referenced journal article. It might be an amazing learning experience to read and discuss different perspectives from a variety of people vested in a topic. This, however, is not the same as spending time reading, analyzing, and discussing published research. Luckily, there's nothing stopping you from doing both!

Presenting at conferences offers another way to share your content, insights, and perspectives with people who tend to shy away from social media and other digital content. Every moment in every presentation attended is another step toward 22, but the real power of the conference happens between the sessions. Every conversation with others can be The One that pushes the needle to 22. And when you return to your agency, develop a plan for sharing your takeaways from the conference with others.

Lead by Sharing with the World

Congratulations! You've created something! Maybe it is a presentation to hook some students. Maybe it is a video describing a concept. Maybe it is a one-pager that describes how to use a tool. Maybe it is an interactive lesson that students can choose to explore on their own. Maybe it is an infographic that gives details about a topic. Whatever you've created, the next step is to ask, "With whom can this be shared?"

Ask yourself if there is any reason you can't share your creation with the widest audience possible. Certain restrictions, such as confidentiality, copyright, and digital-rights permissions (like photo releases) might prevent you from expanding your audience. If those restrictions don't exist, however, lead by sharing with the world!

AWESOME INSIGHT

If more than one person in your agency is attending the same conference, challenge yourselves to spread out! Resist the urge to cluster together. Instead, make a concerted effort to meet different people. Every moment spent with people from your agency is a potential opportunity lost when it comes to learning and connecting with others from outside your agency. There will be plenty of time when you return home to compare notes on what you learned.

When possible, place your creation on the internet in a front-facing fashion. In other words, post it in a way that can be discovered by anyone rather than hiding it behind a password or on an internal server. There are others beyond the confines of the local educational agency who could benefit from your work, and, in turn, you can benefit from the work of others. Contemporary education is as much about sharing resources as it is about learning. We all empower one another when we openly share our knowledge and experience with as many people as possible.

Sharing what works (and what doesn't) isn't just a good idea; it's an obligation of contemporary educational practice. If students of all abilities are expected to learn how to become proficient communicators and collaborators, they need models from whom to learn. A professional responsibility of contemporary educational practice is to connect with other educators locally, regionally, nationally, and globally.

Connections include two-way communications between professionals in which ideas are shared.

The world needs to hear your experiences with tools, strategies, interventions, and techniques that you have found useful. Equally valuable are experiences with supports that have proven to be less than successful in your practice.

Share Little Moments of Awesome

If we educational experience designers, accessible-design facilitators, and everyone else in education are obligated to share, the question that naturally follows is, "What should I share?" And if you are feeling self-conscious or insecure about what to share, you may be asking, "What do I have to share that is of value?" But that's just the little imp of self-doubt whispering on your shoulder. All you need is a little encouragement.

When in doubt or just because, share the little moments of awesome that educators experience every day. These include smiles, connections, creations, products, changes, and breakthroughs. If it is remotely possible that someone else might consider a moment as awesome, share it! Here are some examples:

- Student successes
- Student creations
- Peer connections
- Personal "Aha!" moments
- Intriguing research
- Growth moments (including risks that failed)
- Insights gleaned
- Things you'd improve
- Technology used

Measuring Success with Metrics

The impact of professional development is as difficult to measure as the benefits of technology implementation for a student. In both cases, measure the success by creating a goal. Then measure the progress toward that goal.

When building a program or when asked to justify existing programs, metrics tell the story of how professional-development experiences have been designed and delivered to support (and hopefully meet) the goals of the district. Some vectors to measure include the following:

- Total number of PD experiences offered

- Total number of different types of PD experiences offered

- Total number of different types of PD experiences offered per content-specific area or domain

- Total number of website hits

- Total number of videos viewed on the website

- Total number of downloads from the website

- Total number of website subscribers

- Total number of online friends or followers

- Total number of educators reached

- Total number of students who have reached their goals

- Total number of goals in IEPs mastered

To analyze and then report the data, the data needs to be collected. Keep track of every provision of assistance, professional-development initiative, and any other service provided. Develop an online survey for accessible-design facilitators and/or others providing assistance and conducting PD experiences, like a Google Form or a shared spreadsheet, to collect and maintain data. Collect the data in real time so that when it comes time to analyze and share the story, you'll be ready. Draft a narrative that demonstrates how and where your actions are delivering the desired impact.

Moving Forward

Education should be an enjoyable endeavor for every single student, regardless of ability. As an educator, it is our responsibility to make that doctrine true.

This book is intended to guide you through the process of transforming teachers into educational experience designers who work with accessible-design facilitators to make decisions about which tasks and technologies can be used to shape positive and inclusive learning experiences for everyone.

Use these concepts to help you shape your own practice and the practice of your agency. Embrace the opportunities that contemporary educational philosophies such as Personalized Learning, Universal Design for Learning, Project-Based Learning, and Growth Mindset offer students with disabilities. Become champions for their implementation.

Brand (or rebrand) your service-delivery model around accessible and inclusive design, not assistive technology. Realize that technology is meant to support initiatives and services, not be an initiative or service on its own. Design your service delivery around the principle that everyone knows something about technology that can support students with disabilities.

Everyone involved in the education of a student has a part to play in the consideration and determination of technology. Use the processes outlined here to help guide consistent consideration of least restrictive tools and strategies. When stuck, provide a structure that empowers these individuals to get the assistance they need efficiently and effectively.

Recognize that the content in this book is not exclusive to students in special education. The philosophies, principles, and practices meant to assist students with disabilities apply to *every* student, regardless of ability. It fits everyone.

This book was created to help you build a practice, a perspective, and (if possible) a program based around the principles of designing—not retrofitting—accessible experiences. Whether you're designing a classroom experience, a professional-development workshop, or an entire program on improving the accessibility of your agency, you can't make progress without drafting a prototype. No great design was born perfect, and it often takes failure after failure to know what works and what doesn't.

Try different things often and keep trying when things don't go as planned—keep trying until something sticks. You won't get it right the first time, but every experience is an opportunity for you to change and grow. And even though you might meet your educational goals, the endeavor doesn't stop there; there will always be the next set of problems to solve, the next thing to learn, the expanding to do, and the trying of something new.

This book was meant to prepare you for your journey. Now it's up to you to take the next step on this evolutionary road. Good luck, and remember to have fun!

References

Baker, B., Hill, K., & Devylder, R. (2000). *Core vocabulary is the same across environments.* Paper presented at a meeting of the Technology and Persons with Disabilities Conference at California State University, Northridge.

Bugaj, C., & Norton-Darr, S. (2014). *Practical (and fun) guide to assistive technology in public schools: Building or improving your district's AT team.* Eugene, OR: International Society for Technology in Education.

Bugaj, C. & Poss, B. (2016). Multiple means of measurement: Tools for collecting and analyzing evidence of student progress. *Assistive Technology Outcomes and Benefits, 10,* 37–49.

Donnellan, A. (1984). The criterion of the least dangerous assumption. *Behavioral Disorders, 9*(2), 141–150.

Dweck, C. S. (2017). *Mindset: Changing the way you think to fulfill your potential.* London, England: Robinson.

ESSA (2015). Every Student Succeeds Act of 2015, Pub. L. No. 114-95 § 129 Stat. 1825 (2015–2016).

Finke, E. H., Davis, J. M., Benedict, M., Goga, L., Kelly, J., Palumbo, L., Peart, T., Waters, S. (2017). Effects of a least-to-most prompting procedure on multisymbol message production in children with autism spectrum disorder who use augmentative and alternative communication. *American Journal of Speech-Language Pathology, 26*(1), 81. doi:10.1044/2016_ajslp-14-0187

Frayer, D., Frederick, W. C., & Klausmeier, H. J. (1969). *A schema for testing the level of cognitive mastery.* (Working Report No. 16). Madison, WI: Wisconsin Research and Development Center for Cognitive Learning.

Gollwitzer, P. M., Sheeran, P., Michalski, V., & Seifert, A. E. (2009). When intentions go public. *Psychological Science, 20*(5), 612–618. doi:10.1111/j.1467-9280.2009.02336.x.

IDEA (2004). Individuals with Disabilities Education Improvement Act of 2004, Pub. L. No. 108-446 § 602 Stat. 2652.

Jorgensen, C. (2005). The least dangerous assumption: A challenge to create a new paradigm. *Disability Solutions, 6*(3), 1, 5–9.

Lange, A. A., McPhillips, M., Mulhern, G. & Wylie, J. (2006). Assistive software tools for secondary-level students with literacy difficulties. *Journal of Special Education Technology, 21*(3), 13–22. https://doi.org/10.1177/016264340602100302

McLeskey, J., Tyler, N. C., & Flippin, S. S. (2004). The supply of and demand for special education teachers. *The Journal of Special Education, 38*(1), 5–21. doi:10.1177/00224669040380010201

Mezei, P. J. & Heller, K. W. (2009). *Effects of word prediction on writing fluency for students with physical disabilities* (Unpublished doctoral dissertation, Georgia State University). Retrieved from files.eric.ed.gov/fulltext/EJ986388.pdf

National Center on Accessible Educational Materials (2013). *PALM initiative all-in-one*. Retrieved from www.aem.cast.org/about/publications/2013/purchase-accessible-learning-materials-palm-initiative.html

National Center for Education Statistics (n.d.). Fast facts: Students with disabilities; How many students with disabilities receive services? Retrieved from https://nces.ed.gov/fastfacts/display.asp?id=64

Reed, P., & Gierach, J (2009). Assessing students' needs for assistive technology. Retrieved from www.wati.org/free-publications/assessing-students-needs-for-assistive-technology

Rosenthal, R., & Fode, K. (1963). The effect of experimenter bias on the performance of the albino rat. *Behavioral Science, 8,* 183–189.

Rosenthal, R., &. Jacobson, L. (1966). Teachers' expectancies: Determinants of pupils' IQ gains. *Psychological Reports, 19,* 115–118.

Zabala, J. S.. (n.d.). Sharing the SETT framework. Retrieved from joyzabala.com

Index

A

AAC devices. *See* augmentative/alternative communication (AAC) devices
abilities, student, 183–184
"able to" challenge, 61–64
accessible-design facilitators (ADFs)
    as coaches, 134
    justifying need for, 134–138
    need for, 130
    responsibilities, 132–133
    service-delivery progress report, sample, 191–193
    SETT Framework, 133
accessible-design teams, 140–141
accommodations
    online content versus, 74–75
    turning functions into, 104–106
    wording of suggested, 182
action plan. *See* plan of action
action steps, 217–218
ADFs. *See* accessible-design facilitators (ADFs)
advice, expert, 179
agenda books, 118–120
aided language stimulation, 114
Assessing Students' Needs for Assistive Technology, 154
assessment
    evaluating *versus*, 154
    features for larger student population, 197–200
    summative, 115–116
    text-to-speech tools, 204–205
assistance, documenting
    considerations, 178–179, 189–191
    documentation, sample, 183–188
    elements of documentation, 173
    facts versus opinions, 176–178
    features, optional, 180–183
    importance of, 171–173
    means, multiple, 174–176

    service-delivery progress report, sample, 191–193
    superhero metaphor, 173–174
    Ticket to Ride analogy, 193
assistance, providers of, 146–148, 189–190
assistance, providing
    documentation, reviewing, 163
    evidence, collecting, 168–169
    IEP path, 191
    new things, trying, 163, 166–168
    RIOT functions, 162–168
    stakeholders, interviewing, 163–165
    students, observing, 163, 166
assistance, requesting
    barriers, eliminating, 152–153
    costs, hidden, 157–159
    IEP, sample requests for assistance in, 156
    IEP meeting, during, 153–156
    IEP meeting, prior to, 150–152
    informally, 148–149
    scenarios, 150–152
    synergistic value of, 159
assistance, statement of everlasting, 180–181
assistive technology, as term, 86
Assistive Technology Act (1998), 82
assistive technology devices. *See also specific topics*
    defined, 80, 83–84
    re-envisioning definition, 84–87
assistive technology services, defined, 81
assists in sports, 178
assumptions, 56–58
audio, recording, 110
augmentative/alternative communication (AAC) devices
    communication-partner training materials, 44
    documentation, sample, 183–188
    impact of, 89–91
    least restrictive environment, 114–115, 121–125